Nonnative Fishes in the Upper Mississippi River System

By Kevin S. Irons, Steven A. DeLain, Eric Gittinger, Brian S. Ickes, Cindy S. Kolar, David Ostendorf, Eric N. Ratcliff, and Amy J. Benson

Edited by Kevin S. Irons

Prepared by the Long Term Resource Monitoring Program with science direction from the USGS Upper Midwest Environmental Sciences Center in cooperation with the U.S. Army Corps of Engineers, Rock Island District

Scientific Investigations Report 2009–5176

U.S. Department of the Interior
U.S. Geological Survey

U.S. Department of the Interior
KEN SALAZAR, Secretary

U.S. Geological Survey
Suzette M. Kimball, Acting Director

U.S. Geological Survey, Reston, Virginia: 2009

For more information on the USGS—the Federal source for science about the Earth, its natural and living resources, natural hazards, and the environment, visit http://www.usgs.gov or call 1-888-ASK-USGS

For an overview of USGS information products, including maps, imagery, and publications, visit http://www.usgs.gov/pubprod

To order this and other USGS information products, visit http://store.usgs.gov

Suggested citation:
Irons, K.S., DeLain, S.A., Gittinger, E., Ickes, B.S., Kolar, C.S., Ostendorf, D., Ratcliff, E.N., and Benson, A.J., 2009, Nonnative fishes in the Upper Mississippi River System: U.S. Geological Survey Scientific Investigations Report 2009–5176, 68 p.

Contents

Figures

Tables

Conversion Factors and Abbreviations

Multiply	By	To obtain
centimeter (cm)	0.3937	inch (in.)
millimeter (mm)	0.03937	inch (in.)
meter (m)	3.281	foot (ft)
meter (m)	1.094	yard (yd)
kilometer (km)	0.6214	mile (mi)
kilometer (km)	0.5400	mile, nautical (nmi)
mile (mi)	1.609	kilometer (km)
square kilometer (km^2)	247.1	acre
gram (g)	0.03527	ounce, avoirdupois (oz)
kilogram (kg)	2.205	pound avoirdupois (lb)
metric ton	1.102	ton

Temperature in degrees Celsius (°C) may be converted to degrees Fahrenheit (°F) as follows:

°F=(1.8×°C)+32

μm, micrometer: a micrometer is one millionth of a meter or one thousandth of a millimeter.

Acknowledgments

This study was funded by the U.S. Army Corp of Engineers as part of the Long Term Resource Monitoring Program (LTRMP) with program guidance and support provided by the U.S. Geological Survey, Upper Midwest Environmental Sciences Center (UMESC). The data used to prepare this report was collected by staff from the Iowa Department of Natural Resources, Illinois Natural History Survey, Minnesota Department of Natural Resources, Missouri Department of Conservation, and Wisconsin Department of Natural Resources. We thank all of the people who contributed to this report. Specifically, we thank Jennifer S. Sauer, Barry L. Johnson, Elizabeth A. Ciganovich, Georginia R. Ardinger, and the anonymous reviewers for their exceptional work and helpful comments in the final preparation of this manuscript. Finally, the authors would like to thank the countless people who have contributed to the LTRMP efforts over the years, as well as those dedicated to maintaining long term monitoring of the Upper Mississippi River System.

Nonnative Fishes in the Upper Mississippi River System

By Kevin S. Irons[1], Steven A. DeLain[2], Eric Gittinger[3], Brian S. Ickes[4], Cindy S. Kolar[4], David Ostendorf[5], Eric N. Ratcliff[3], and Amy J. Benson[6]

Abstract

The introduction, spread, and establishment of nonnative species is widely regarded as a leading threat to aquatic biodiversity and consequently is ranked among the most serious environmental problems facing the United States today. This report presents information on nonnative fish species observed by the Long Term Resource Monitoring Program on the Upper Mississippi River System a nexus of North American freshwater fish diversity for the Nation. The Long Term Resource Monitoring Program, as part of the U.S. Army Corps of Engineers' Environmental Management Plan, is the Nation's largest river monitoring program and stands as the primary source of standardized ecological information on the Upper Mississippi River System. The Long Term Resource Monitoring Program has been monitoring fish communities in six study areas on the Upper Mississippi River System since 1989. During this period, more than 3.5 million individual fish, consisting of 139 species, have been collected. Although fish monitoring activities of the Long Term Resource Monitoring Program focus principally on entire fish communities, data collected by the Program are useful for detecting and monitoring the establishment and spread of nonnative fish species within the Upper Mississippi River System Basin. Sixteen taxa of nonnative fishes, or hybrids thereof, have been observed by the Long Term Resource Monitoring Program since 1989, and several species are presently expanding their distribution and increasing in abundance. For example, in one of the six study areas monitored by the Long Term Resource Monitoring Program, the number of established nonnative species has increased from two to eight species in less than 10 years. Furthermore, contributions of those eight species can account for up to 60 percent of the total annual catch and greater than 80 percent of the observed biomass. These observations are critical because the Upper Mississippi River System stands as a nationally significant pathway for nonnative species expansion between the Mississippi River and the Great Lakes Basin. This report presents a synthesis of data on nonnative fish species observed during Long Term Resource Monitoring Program monitoring activities.

Introduction

The spread and impact of nonnative species have recently been described as perhaps the least reversible human-induced change under way in ecosystems worldwide (Kolar and Lodge, 2002) and are among the most serious environmental problems facing the 21st century (Mooney and Hobbs, 2000; Carlton, 2001). The prevention, control, and mitigation of the impacts of some harmful nonnative species are economically costly. One report, for example, estimates that the economic cost of invasive species to Americans is $137 billion every year (Pimentel and others, 2000). This estimate surely underestimates the true cost of harmful nonnative species, because it includes only those damages for which market values exist. In addition, harmful nonnative species can negatively impact native species in the ecosystems they invade. For instance, up to 46 percent of the plants and animals listed as federally endangered species have been negatively impacted by invasive species (Wilcove and others, 1998). Nonnative species and habitat degradation are routinely ranked as the top two threats to aquatic biodiversity (Allan and Flecker, 1993; Sala and others, 2000; Tockner and Stanford, 2002).

For the purpose of this report, a nonnative species is a species found outside of its native range. Although some nonnative species are not native anywhere in the United States, others have been introduced from where they are native within the country to other portions of the country, for example, from one watershed to another. Most established nonnative species are not necessarily considered a nuisance. Nuisance species typically spread quickly throughout ecosystems, become abundant, and are perceived by humans as having a negative impact. It has been suggested that perhaps 10 percent of nonnative species fall into this problematic category (Williamson, 1996). Furthermore, a nonnative species is sometimes considered "invasive," meaning that it has negative impacts that

[1] Illinois Natural History Survey, Illinois River Biological Station, 704 N. Schrader Ave., Havana, IL 62644; email: kirons@staff.uiuc.edu

[2] Minnesota Department of Natural Resources, Lake City Field Station, 1801 South Oak Street, Lake City, MN 55041

[3] Illinois Natural History Survey, Great Rivers Field Station, 8450 Montclair, Brighton, IL 62012

[4] U.S. Geological Survey, Upper Midwest Environmental Sciences Center, 2630 Fanta Reed Road, La Crosse, WI 54603

[5] Missouri Department of Conservation, Open River Field Station, 3815 East Jackson Boulevard, Jackson, MO 63755

[6] U.S. Geological Survey, 7920 NW 71st Street, Gainesville, FL 32653

outweigh potential positive environmental or economic values. In this report, nonnative species will be presented regardless of their perceived effect on the environment or economy, although this issue may be discussed for particular taxa.

Nonnative Fish Species in the Upper Mississippi River System

Home to approximately 25 percent of North American species (about 150 of an estimated 600 species), the Upper Mississippi River System (fig. 1) is the nexus of freshwater fish biodiversity on the continent. Mills and others (1966) noted that 10.9 metric tons of the commercially harvested fish of the United States came from the Illinois River alone in 1908. It was noted by Alvord and Burdick (1919) that only the Great Lakes and Pacific salmon fisheries surpassed this Illinois River fishery. Remarkably, this high harvest in the early part of the 20th century was due largely to the introduction of one nonnative fish species, the common carp *Cyprinus carpio*, and diversion of Lake Michigan water through the Chicago Sanitary and Ship Canal (Mills and others, 1966). However, the modern-day spread of additional nonnative species threatens the phenomenal biodiversity of freshwater fishes in the Upper Mississippi River System.

A 1997 survey of member states of the Mississippi Interstate Conservation Resources Association found that 163 nonnative species are established in the Mississippi River Basin (Rasmussen, 2002). With 83 species, more nonnative fishes were reported than any other taxon as being established in the Mississippi River Basin (62 plants, 16 invertebrates, 1 amphibian, and 1 mammal were also listed). According to the 1997 Mississippi Interstate Conservation Resources Association survey, only 17 percent of the reported nonnative species are presently found in the states that comprise the Upper Mississippi River System (Rasmussen, 2002). The survey indicated that, with 163 species, the number of established nonnative species in the Mississippi River Basin is nearly identical to the number of those established in the Great Lakes (162 species; Ricciardi, 2001), an ecosystem often described as highly altered by many invasions of nonnative species. Furthermore, the U.S. Geological Survey has documented 85 nonnative taxa (species and hybrids) within the Upper Mississippi River System alone [U.S. Geological Survey, 2004, Nonindigenous Aquatic Species database online at *http://nas. er.usgs.gov/*]. Many of these records document failed introductions of nonnative species that nonetheless were once present within a basin.

Before the 1970s, the common carp was the only nonnative fish species that had become abundant in the Upper Mississippi River System and probably the only species to have been considered a nuisance. Since 1970, however, five out of the nine fishes that have become established in the Upper Mississippi River System have quickly become abundant, and

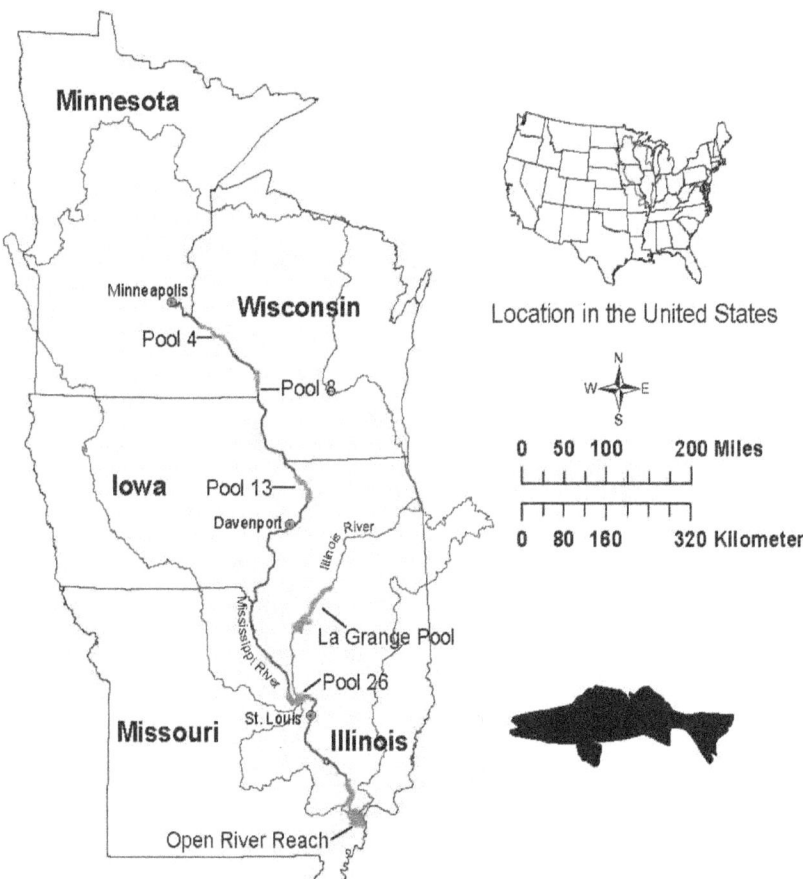

Figure 1. The Upper Mississippi River System, as defined by Public Law 99-662, is the commercially navigable reaches of the Mississippi, Illinois, Minnesota, Black, Saint Croix, and Kaskaskia Rivers. The System essentially includes rivers draining into the Mississippi River above the confluence of the Ohio River, excluding the Missouri River, and drains approximately 490,000 square kilometers of five Midwestern states. The Long Term Resource Monitoring Program monitors 6 study areas within this System, five on the Mississippi River and one on the Illinois River

they are either considered a nuisance or concern exists about their potential nuisance status. This shift in establishment of more high impact nonnative fishes, along with the increasing rate of invasion in the Upper Mississippi River System, further indicates the need to better understand the mechanisms of introduction, establishment, spread, and impact of nonnative fishes in the ecosystem. Analysis of long-term fish catch data of sufficient scale to detect many of the nonnative fish species can begin to help develop this understanding.

Fish Monitoring by the Long Term Resource Monitoring Program

The U.S. Congress recognized the Upper Mississippi River System as both a nationally significant ecosystem and a nationally significant commercial navigation system (The Upper Mississippi River Management Act of 1986, Public Law 99–662, sec. 1103). An Environmental Management Plan was developed and authorized by the Water Resources Development Act in 1986, as a result of the emphasis on sustaining both the economic and environmental benefits of this resource. As part of this Plan, the Long Term Resource Monitoring Program was developed as a cooperative effort between the five states bordering the Upper Mississippi River System, the U.S. Geological Survey, and the U.S. Army Corps of Engineers (U.S. Geological Survey, 1999).

The mission of the Long Term Resource Monitoring Program is to provide resource managers and decision makers with information necessary to maintain the Upper Mississippi River System as a sustainable multiple-use large river ecosystem. The long-term goals of the Program were established through extensive Federal and state agency participation and include: (1) developing a better understanding of the ecology of the Upper Mississippi River System and its resource problems, (2) monitoring resource change, (3) developing alternatives to better manage the Upper Mississippi River System, and (4) providing for the proper management of Long Term Resource Monitoring Program information. In meeting the goals of the program, it is imperative to summarize data on nonnative species as they appear within the sampling areas.

Study Area and Methods

Fisheries monitoring began in 1989 as part of the Long Term Resource Monitoring Program. In 1990, standardized monitoring was completed in five of six study reaches (Pools 4, 8, 13, and 26 of the Mississippi River, and La Grange Reach of the Illinois River). Monitoring in the Open River Reach of the Mississippi River began in 1991 (Gutreuter and others, 1995; Gutreuter, 1997). These reaches have been selected, in part, to represent the diversity in geomorphology, land use, and habitat availability, as well as navigational management strategies within the Upper Mississippi River System (Gutreuter, 1997). In brief, monitoring on these reaches was conducted with multiple sampling methods and gear types

(boat electrofishing, fyke nets, hoop nets, seining, trawling, gill nets, and trammel nets) in various habitats (backwater lakes, side channels, main channel, tailwater zones) of the Upper Mississippi River System and by use of a statistical sampling design and standard sampling protocol. Sampling effort varied among study reaches, habitats, and gears. Monitoring design changed significantly in 1993. Generally, fixed sites sampled before 1993 were subjectively selected by project biologists to represent major river habitats. From 1993 to present, sites are randomly selected with the aid of a geographical information system that is stratified by basic habitat units. In addition, a few fixed sites remained at various pools in years following the change to stratified random sampling. Therefore, care needs to be taken when comparing data across years due to sampling effort and yearly gear efficiency issues. Additional information can be found on the Web site of the Upper Midwest Environmental Sciences Center (*http:\\www. umesc.usgs.gov/*) or various program publications including the Long Term Resource Monitoring Program Fish Procedures Manual (Gutreuter and others, 1995, 1997a–e; Burkhardt and others, 1997, 1998, 2000, 2001).

Summary of Nonnative Fish Monitoring Data from 1989 to 2002

Monitoring activities conducted within the six Long Term Resource Monitoring Program study areas from 1989 to 2002 resulted in the collection of more than 31,000 samples and more than 4.3 million fish consisting of 139 species. Of these, 12 species (8.6 percent) are considered nonnative in the basin. Compared with some other large river systems, the proportion of nonnative species within the Upper Mississippi River System is relatively low. For example, 79 percent of the species in the Colorado River, 38 percent in the Columbia River, and 21 percent in the Rhine River are nonnative species (Galat and Zweimueller, 2001).

Nonnative fish species accounted for 7.6 percent of the total number of fish collected from 1989 to 2002 by the Long Term Resource Monitoring Program, although substantial variability exists among years. For example, large catches of threadfin shad *Dorosoma petenense* in 1991 and 2001, primarily from La Grange Reach, inflated the total annual percentage to 15–27 percent (fig. 2). Similarly, large catches of common carp increased the annual total to 11 percent in 1994 (fig. 2). Even though the percentage of nonnative fish in Program collections was low, these data also showed that in most study reaches more than 30 percent of the biomass of annual fish collections were nonnative species, primarily common carp, which is a large bodied cyprinid (minnow) (fig. 3). Because bighead *Hypophthalmichthys nobilis* and silver *H. molitrix* carp (other large bodied cyprinids) are presently expanding their range within the basin, it is conceivable that the biomass of nonnative fish in the Upper Mississippi River System will increase in the future.

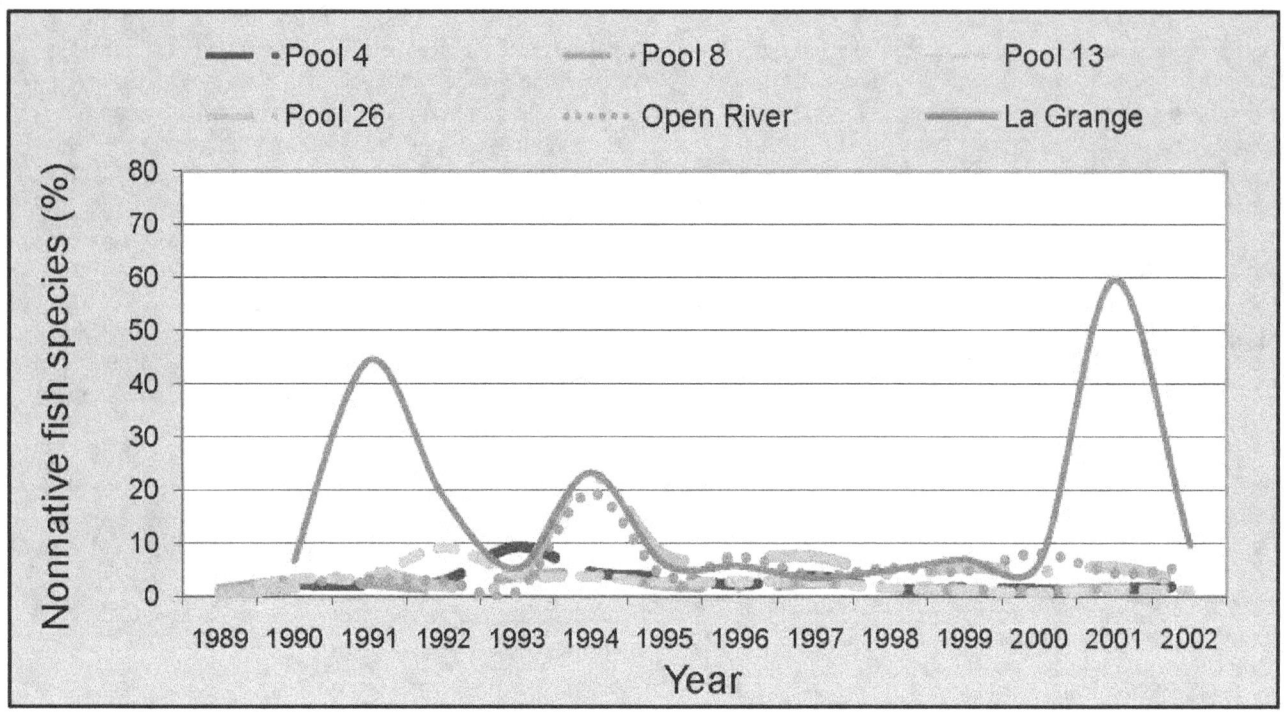

Figure 2.   Percentage of nonnative fish species in the total number of fish collected annually from 1989 to 2002 by the Long Term Resource Monitoring Program.

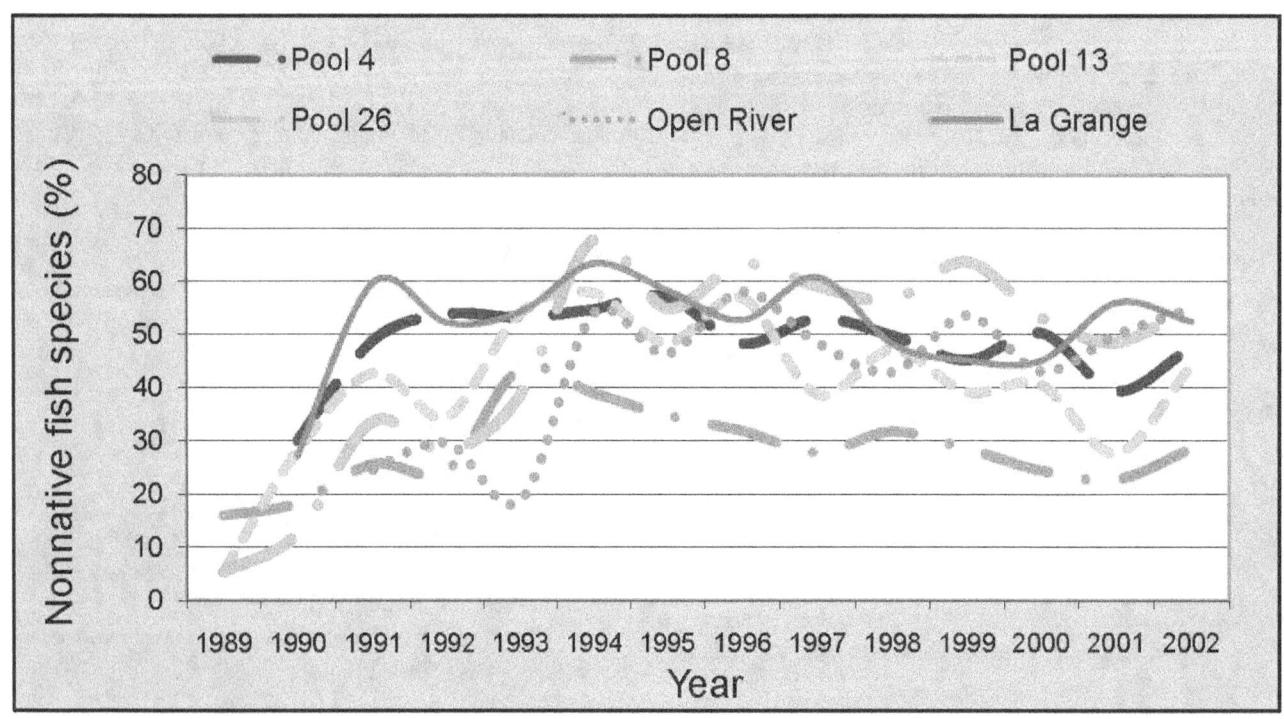

Figure 3.   Percentage of total biomass of nonnative fish species in the total biomass of fish collected annually from 1989 to 2002 by the Long Term Resource Monitoring Program.

Several nonnative species in the Upper Mississippi River System hybridize with native taxa, either naturally or as part of stocking programs for creating recreational angling opportunities. Four taxa have appeared in Long Term Resource Monitoring Program fish collections that are hybrids with nonnative species: common carp x goldfish *Cyprinus carpio x Carassius auratus*, tiger muskellunge *Esox masquinongy* x *E. lucius*, striped bass or wiper *Morone saxatilis* x *M. chrysops*, and hybrid white perch *M. americana* x *M. mississippiensis*. Therefore, 12 nonnative species and 4 associated hybrids constitute 16 nonnative fishes that have been collected by the Long Term Resource Monitoring Program in the Upper Mississippi River System (table 1).

Several additional nonnative fishes are either poised to enter the Upper Mississippi River System or have recently been observed in the system, but have not been detected by Long Term Resource Monitoring Program sampling. Both the black carp *Mylopharyngodon piceus* and giant snakehead *Channa micropeltes* were collected in the Upper Mississippi

River System in 2003 for the first time (fig. 4*A*, *B*). In addition, round goby *Neogobius melanostomus* have been collected by other agencies in the Calumet and Des Plaines Rivers, in the upper reaches of the Illinois River watershed, since 1993, and round goby were caught in a trawl by Long Term Resource Monitoring Program monitoring in La Grange Reach, Illinois River, in summer 2004 (Irons and others, 2006.)

Black carp were first imported into the United States accidentally in grass carp *Ctenopharyngodon idella* stocks used in aquaculture operations (Nico and others, 2005). Later, they were stocked intentionally as a food fish and to control yellow grub infestations in channel catfish *Ictalurus punctatus* aquaculture operations. In 1994, 30 or more black carp escaped into the Osage River, a tributary of the Missouri River (Nico and others, 2005). No specimens were caught in the wild until March 26, 2003, when a 4-year-old black carp was caught by a commercial fisher in Horseshoe Lake, Alexander County, Ill. Scientists and natural resource managers are

Table 1. Sixteen nonnative fish taxa (species and hybrids) collected by the Long Term Resource Monitoring Program monitoring of the Upper Mississippi River System from 1989 to 2002.

[*Indicates taxa only discussed in chapter of parental species.]

Common Name	Family	Genus species	Year first detected
Threadfin shad	Clupeidae	*Dorosoma petenense*	1989
Goldfish	Cyprinidae	*Carassius auratus*	1989
Grass carp	Cyprinidae	*Ctenopharyngodon idella*	1991
Common carp	Cyprinidae	*Cyprinus carpio*	1989
Carp x goldfish hybrid*	Cyprinidae	*Cyprinus carpio* x *auratus*	1990
Silver carp	Cyprinidae	*Hypopthalmichthys molitrix*	1998
Bighead carp	Cyprinidae	*Hypopthalmichthys nobilis*	1991
Rudd	Cyprinidae	*Scardinius erythrophthalmus*	2002
Muskellunge	Esocidae	*Esox masquinongy*	1996
Tiger muskellunge	Esocidae	*Esox masquinongy* x *lucius*	1992
Rainbow smelt	Osmeridae	*Osmerus mordax*	1993
Brown trout	Salmonidae	*Salmo trutta*	1992
White perch	Percichthyidae	*Morone americana*	1992
White perch x yellow bass*	Percichthyidae	*M. american* x *mississippiensis*	2001
Striped bass	Percichthyidae	*Morone saxatilis*	1991
Striped bass x white bass	Percichthyidae	*M. saxatilis* x *chrysops*	1993

concerned that black carp may become established in the Upper Mississippi River System, and the U.S. Fish and Wildlife Service is presently considering listing black carp as an injurious species. Black carp are molluscivores, and, therefore, a threat to freshwater mussel populations, which are one of the most endangered groups of aquatic biota in North America (Master and others, 2000). Several more black carp have been collected throughout the Mississippi River System since 2003 (U.S. Geological Survey, 2004, NAS database online at *http://nas.er.usgs.gov/*).

The giant snakehead was collected in the Rock River, Wis., a tributary of the Upper Mississippi River System, during a Wisconsin Department of Natural Resources survey in September 2003. The fish, initially identified as a native bowfin *Amia calva*, was 61 cm in length (Wisconsin Department of Natural Resources, written commun., 2004). The giant snakehead was most likely released by a home aquarist. If this large predator were to become established in the Upper Mississippi River System, it could prey on many native fishes. Although the giant snakehead would not normally survive winter temperatures at Upper Mississippi River System latitudes, warm water discharges, such as those from power plants, which occur at many locations throughout the system provide suitable winter refuge.

The round goby, introduced from Eurasia by released ballast water from commercial ships in the Great Lakes, has slowly been expanding its population down the Calumet and Des Planes Rivers toward the Illinois and Mississippi Rivers since 1993. This benthic fish is likely to affect native sculpin species and other benthic fishes as its range expands further (Laird and Page, 1996; Irons and others, 2006).

Figure 4.   Three nonnative fish species of concern for the Upper Mississippi River System have not yet been observed by the Long Term Resource Monitoring Program: *A*, black carp *Mylopharyngodon piceus* and. *B*, giant snakehead *Channa micropeltes*. *C*, Round goby *Neogobius melanostomus* was first found in the Upper Mississippi River System in La Grange Reach, Illinois River, during Long Term Monitoring Program sampling during 2004. (*A*, Rob Cosgriff, Illinois Natural History Survey, Great Rivers Biological Station; *B*, Wisconsin Department of Natural Resources; *C*, Kevin Irons, Illinois Natural History Survey, Illinois River Biological Station)

Purpose and Scope

This publication presents detailed information about the nonnative fishes collected by the Long Term Resource Monitoring Program from 1989 to 2002. The information provided in this report can be used to develop targeted monitoring strategies, inform directed research, develop management alternatives for control, and to guide natural resource policies on nonnative species. For each taxon, a photograph, information about the species, and the life history in its native range is presented, and known or suspected pathways of introduction into the Upper Mississippi River System are discussed. Gross distributional patterns within the United States are documented by national maps (top, fig. 5), in which the red shaded areas represent small hydrologic units where each species has been introduced. However, the shaded areas on the maps do not mean that the species is everywhere within that unit; the area shown is a convenient spatial unit to depict introduction of the species on a national scale. Each species is not always established in these red areas; the maps show where introductions have occurred regardless of the fate of the species. The data used to compile the maps were drawn from scientific literature, museum specimens, and numerous personal communications with other biologists and researchers, and it is maintained within the U.S. Geological Survey Nonindigenous Species Database. The Upper Mississippi River System

basin maps were constructed by use of Long Term Resource Monitoring Program station records (bottom, fig. 5). Similar U.S. Geological Survey national maps are available online as part of a World Wide Web site serving as a clearinghouse of nonindigenous aquatic species in the United States (U. S. Geological Survey, 2004, Nonindigenous Aquatic Species database online at *http://nas.er.usgs.gov/*).

Patterns in macrohabitat use are defined, the efficacy of various Long Term Resource Monitoring Program sampling methods for detecting and enumerating the species are identified, temporal and spatial trends in species abundance are depicted, and potential or realized ecological and economic impacts are discussed. All nonnative species collected by the Program are presented in phylogenetic order by family and then alphabetically by scientific name. Common and scientific names of fishes are listed in the Appendix.

White perch x yellow bass hybrids and common carp x goldfish hybrids are discussed within parental species accounts. These hybrids occur because of the presence of the parental species—that is, white perch, common carp, or goldfish—within the system. Dedicated species accounts are presented for tiger muskellunge and hybrid striped bass, because fisheries managers stocked these purposefully and their presence probably is not a result of parental species within the system. Therefore, in-depth information will be presented for 14 taxa.

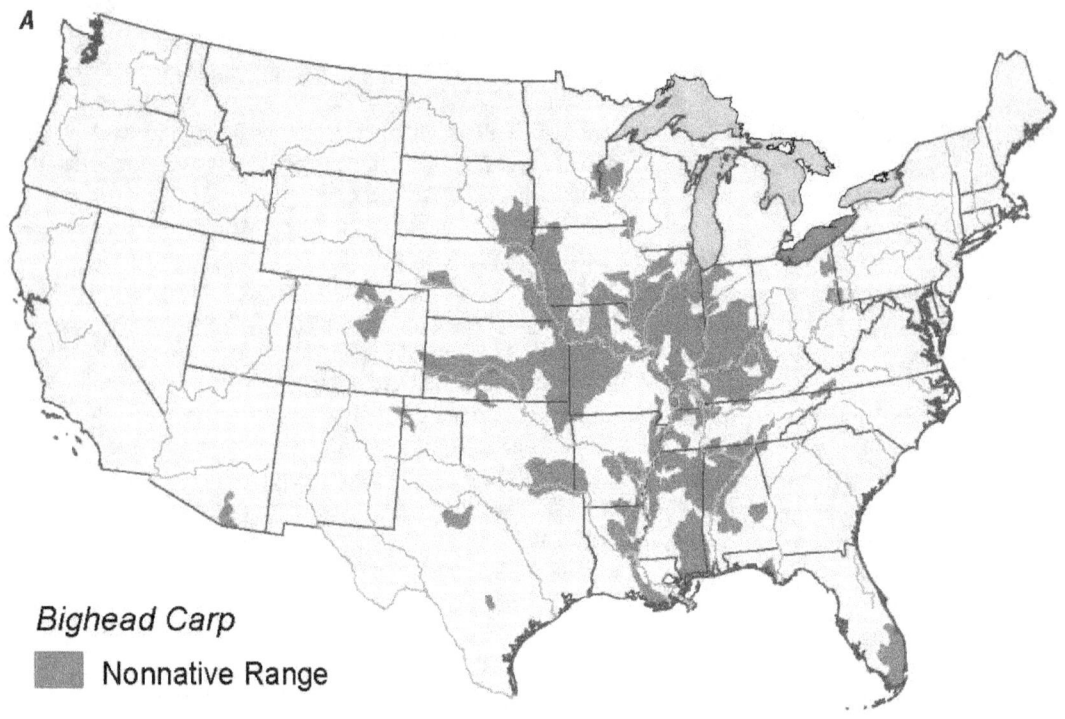

Bighead Carp

Nonnative Range

Figure 5. Examples of *A*, national distribution maps of bighead carp, and *B*, Long Term Resource Monitoring Program catch records of white perch.

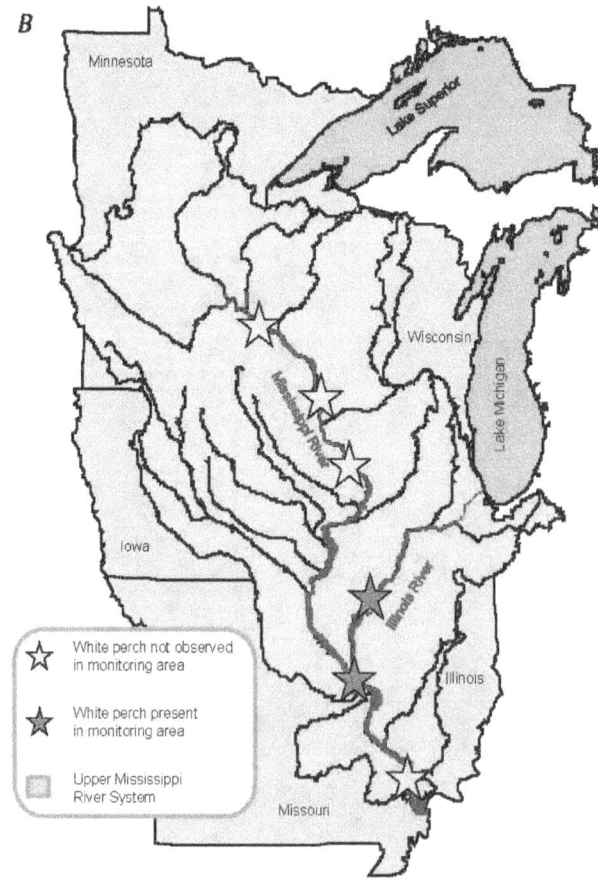

Threadfin Shad *Dorosoma petenense*

Native Range Biology

The threadfin shad is a member of the herring family (Clupeidae). *Dorosoma* is Greek for "lance body," referring to the body shape, and *petenense* refers to Lake Peten in the Yucatan (Guatemala), where the species was first observed (Günther, 1866). Threadfin shad differ from the more common Upper Mississippi River System native gizzard shad by having a terminal mouth. The lower lip of the threadfin shad will be forced open when a finger is slid down the snout, whereas the lower lip of the gizzard shad *Dorosoma cepedianum* will remain closed (Smith, 1979).

Photograph by Kevin Irons, Illinois Natural History Survey, Illinois River Biological Station

Native range of the threadfin shad is somewhat debated. Before 1945, the threadfin shad was found only in rivers and streams flowing into the Gulf of Mexico, from Florida to Mexico (Forbes and Richardson, 1920; Smith, 1979). Later, its range expanded northward (Trautman, 1981). In 1948, threadfin shad were discovered in impoundments of the Tennessee River (Tennessee Valley Authority, 1954), and in 1957 the first Illinois specimens were collected from tributaries of the Ohio River (Minckley and Krumholz, 1960). An alternative opinion is that the threadfin shad was originally found as far south as Belize and was distributed northward into Gulf States as well as states bordering the lower Mississippi and Ohio Rivers, including Illinois and Missouri (Page and Burr, 1991).

Threadfin shad can live longer than 4 years and reach a maximum size of 23 cm in length; however, most do not live longer than 2 years and adults seldom exceed 13 cm in freshwater (Laird and Page, 1996). Threadfin shad do not tolerate cold-water temperatures, showing decreased activity and feeding at 9°C. Griffith (1978) found temperatures of 4°C to be lethal, but Long Term Resource Monitoring Program data suggest that threadfin shad are either more tolerant of low temperatures than previously believed or they have found thermal refuge in this northern part of its current range. For example, water temperatures are less than 4°C for 1 month or more almost every year in Pool 26 of the Mississippi River and La Grange Reach of the Illinois River, yet threadfin shad have been collected every year since 1991 in these study reaches.

Threadfin shad are open-water filter feeders that form large schools. They feed over soft substrates such as sand and mud (Laird and Page, 1996) and are most commonly found in quiet waters such as lakes, oxbows, and pools of large rivers (Smith, 1979). Plankton is their primary energy source, especially in spring and summer (Haskell, 1959). Algae can make up 16–54 percent of their diet (Haskell, 1959; Miller, 1967) and appear to be the primary food source in winter (Haskell, 1959). Threadfin shad also commonly feed on the bottom, which is evident from the mud, sand, and debris found in the gut of most individuals (Miller, 1967).

Threadfin shad typically spawn during spring in water temperatures of 14.4 to 27.2°C for a short period of time at sunrise (Laird and Page, 1996). Separate age classes have been shown to have peak spawns at different times and temperatures, with older fish spawning earlier than the younger fish (Johnson, 1971). Fecundity can range from 1,000 to 25,000 eggs per female, although some females may be capable of spawning more than once per year, suggesting that annual fecundity estimates could be higher (Laird and Page, 1996). The eggs are spherical, 0.75 mm in diameter, and adhesive, sticking to objects such as submerged vegetation, floating debris, bushes, stumps, logs, filamentous algae, rocks, and sticks (Kimsey and Fisk, 1964; Rawstron, 1964; Laird and Page, 1996). The incubation period is 3–6 days, depending on water temperatures (Moyle, 1976).

Threadfin shad larvae are planktonic and exhibit vertical migration through the water column, inhabiting near-surface waters during the day and moving to deeper waters at night (Taber, 1969). Most recent research has shown that threadfin shad reach sexual maturity at age 1 (Johnson, 1971; Laird and Page, 1996), but age-0 fish have been reported to mature (Smith, 1979).

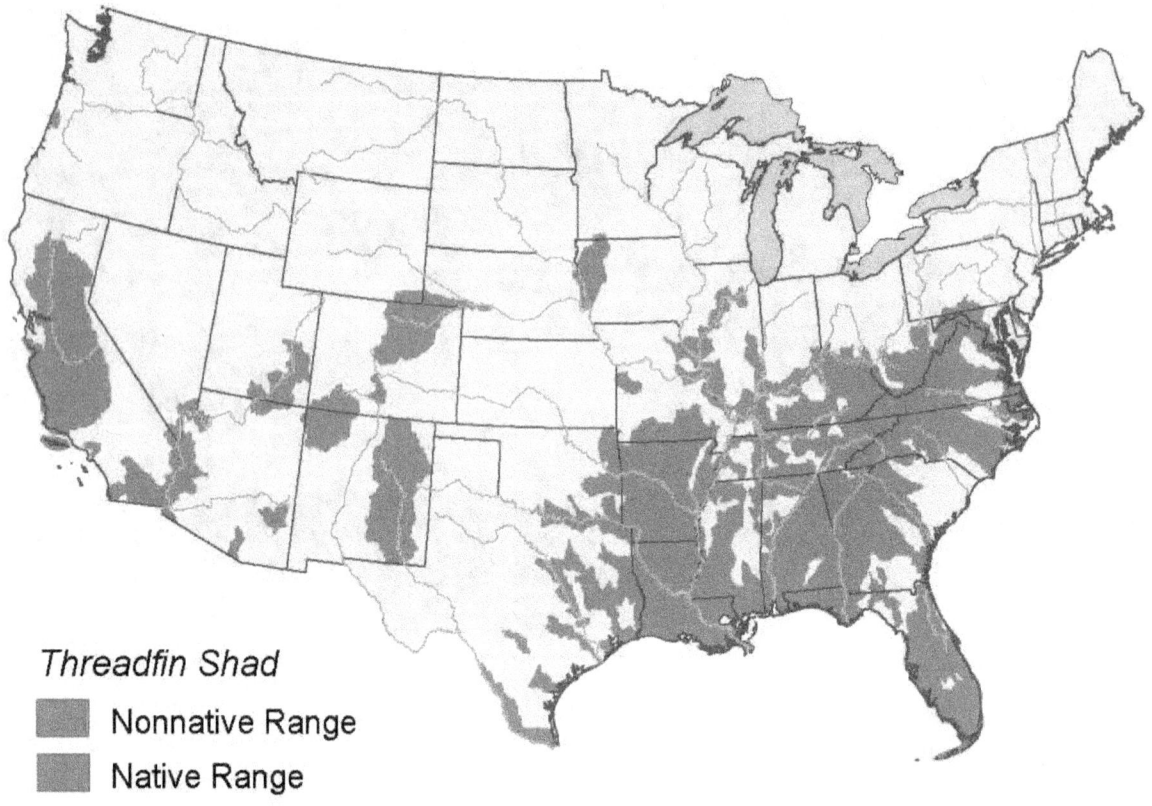

Threadfin Shad

■ Nonnative Range

■ Native Range

Figure 6.   Distribution of threadfin shad *Dorosoma petenense* in the United States.

Pathway of Introduction

Although the extent of the native range of the threadfin shad (fig. 6) is debated, much of the spread of threadfin shad can be attributed to intentional stocking. Threadfin shad are often stocked as a forage base for large predators because of their short life expectancy, relatively small size, and high fecundity (Tomelleri and Eberle, 1990). When threadfin shad escape heated cooling reservoirs into northern rivers, it is likely that warm-water discharges from power plants and industry aid in winter survival.

Distribution in Long Term Resource Monitoring Program Study Reaches

Threadfin shad have been collected from the Open River Reach and Pool 26 of the Mississippi River and La Grange Reach of the Illinois River, all in the most southern part of the Long Term Resource Monitoring Program study area. In the first year of the Program (1989), 32 threadfin shad were collected in Pool 26. In 1991, 414 threadfin shad were collected at both Pool 26 and Open River Reach Field Stations, whereas

La Grange Reach Field Station reported more than 20,000. All three field stations have collected threadfin shad every year since 1991, except for the Open River Reach Field Station in 1997.

Relation of Habitat and Sampling Method to Fish Catch

The Long Term Resource Monitoring Program collections of threadfin shad (fig. 7) were made in all habitat strata. However, they seem to prefer lotic habitats such as tailwater zone, main channel border-unstructured, main channel border-wing dams, and side channel border to the more lentic backwater, contiguous-offshore, backwater, contiguous-shoreline, and impounded habitat-shoreline. These lotic habitats accounted for 85.9 percent of the total catch, whereas the lentic habitats accounted for just 14.1 percent.

Minnow fyke nets were the most successful Long Term Resource Monitoring Program gear for collecting threadfin shad, accounting for 88.9 percent of the total catch for all three field stations. Seines (4.3 percent), fyke nets (3.1 percent), and day electrofishing (2.8 percent) have also caught threadfin combined were from 1991 (14.8 percent), 2001 (70.5 percent) and 2002 (10.8 percent).

In both Pool 26 and the Open River Reach of the Mississippi River, the annual total catch of threadfin shad for 1989–2002 ranged from 0 to 414 individuals and showed no overall trend apparent. Pool 26 Field Station collected 950 threadfin shad, and the Open River Reach Field Station collected 916 threadfin shad during this period.

Ecological Impacts

Because they are a prolific fish that feed on plankton, threadfin shad have the potential to compete for food resources with native fishes in areas of the Upper Mississippi River System where they are not limited by low water temperatures. Native species such as paddlefish, bigmouth buffalo, and gizzard shad all derive energy from plankton food sources throughout their life cycles, and almost all fishes rely on plankton as larvae (Smith, 1979). Dill and Cordone (1997) stated that threadfin shad compete with young sunfishes for food and have destroyed fishing in some areas.

The inability of threadfin shad to tolerate water temperatures below 4°C potentially limits their expansion into new areas of the Upper Mississippi River System. However, factors, such as development that leads to increases in power plant and industrial warmwater discharges and continuing environmental warming trends, may allow the threadfin shad to extend its range further northward in the Upper Mississippi River System.

Discussion

Threadfin shad are, arguably, native to the south-central United States, but are not native to most of the Upper Mississippi River System (Laird and Page, 1996; Pflieger, 1997). The intentional stocking of threadfin shad as a forage fish has greatly expanded their range throughout the Upper Mississippi River System and much of the remainder of the United States. Further range expansion in the Upper Mississippi River System appears to be limited by the inability of threadfin shad to tolerate cold-water temperatures. High fecundity combined with low cold tolerance could explain the "boom and bust" population dynamics observed in Long Term Resource Monitoring Program collections. Because they are planktonic filter feeders, threadfin shad have the potential to compete with the larvae of almost all native species in the Upper Mississippi River System as well as with many adult filter-feeding fishes such as paddlefish, bigmouth buffalo, and gizzard shad. The introduction and expansion of threadfin shad combined with the recent population explosion of nonnative bighead and silver carp may dramatically increase competition for planktonic energy sources in the Upper Mississippi River System.

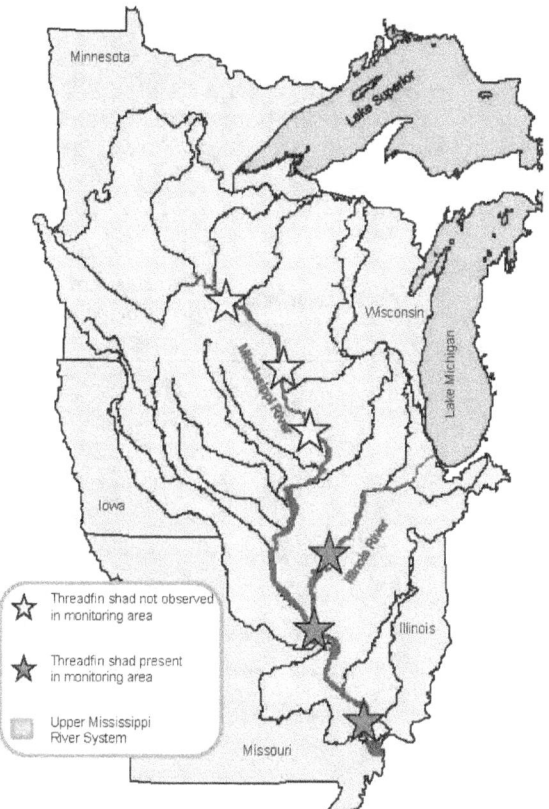

Figure 7. Long Term Resource Monitoring Program study reaches where threadfin shad *Dorosoma petenense* were collected within the Upper Mississippi River System Basin from 1989 to 2002

shad. Minnow fyke nets in the tailwater zone have been the most productive Program gear/habitat combination with 81,076 fish. This accounts for 59 percent of all threadfin shad collected by the Program. Minnow fyke nets set in the side channel border, main channel border-unstructured, and backwater, contiguous-shoreline habitat strata accounted for an additional 39.5 percent of the total threadfin shad catch (table 2).

Trends in Distribution and Abundance

The vast majority (99 percent) of threadfin shad collected by the Long Term Resource Monitoring Program (fig. 8) were from La Grange Reach of the Illinois River during the period 1989–2002. In addition, almost 84,000 unidentified Clupeids were also collected from this reach, potentially increasing the threadfin shad total. Threadfin shad appear to have increased in La Grange Reach from 1989 to 2002; however, there is large variation from year to year. For example, 96 percent of the threadfin shad collected by the Program from all stations

Table 2.   Threadfin shad *Dorosoma petenense* total catch from 1989 to 2002, by strata and gear, from the Long Term Resource Monitoring Program.

[Strata abbreviations: BWC-O, backwater, contiguous-offshore; BWC-S, backwater, contiguous-shoreline; IMP-O, impounded habitat-offshore; IMP-S, impounded habitat-shoreline; MCB-U, main channel border-unstructured; MCB-W, main channel border-wing dams; SCB, side channel border; TRIB, tributary mouth; TWZ, tailwater zone-400 meters below dam. Gear definitions: DEF, day electrofishing; F, fyke net; M, minnow fyke net; NEF, night electrofishing; S, seine; T, trawl; TA, trammel net-anchored; X, tandem fyke net-offshore; Y, tandem minnow fyke net-offshore. —, no catch; NA, not applicable]

| | | Gear | | | | | | | | Total catch, by strata | Percentage of total catch, by strata |
		DEF	F	M	NEF	S	T	X	Y		
Strata	BWC-O	—	—	—	—	—	—	185	411	596	0.4
	BWC-S	513	3,991	13,299	159	312	—	—	—	18,274	13.3
	IMP-O	—	—	—	—	—	—	14	17	31	.0
	IMP-S	244	27	35	—	—	—	—	—	306	.2
	MCB-U	1,588	2	13,290	70	1,613	1	—	—	16,564	12.0
	MCB-W	168	63	56	—	—	—	—	—	287	.2
	SCB	688	16	14,785	106	4,037	—	—	—	19,632	14.2
	TRIB	54	1	22	2	—	—	—	—	79	.1
	TWZ	578	179	81,076	216	—	5	—	—	82,054	59.5
Total catch, by gear		3,833	4,279	122,563	553	5,962	6	199	428	137,823	NA
Percentage of total catch, by gear		2.8	3.1	88.9	0.4	4.3	0.0	0.1	0.3	NA	100.0

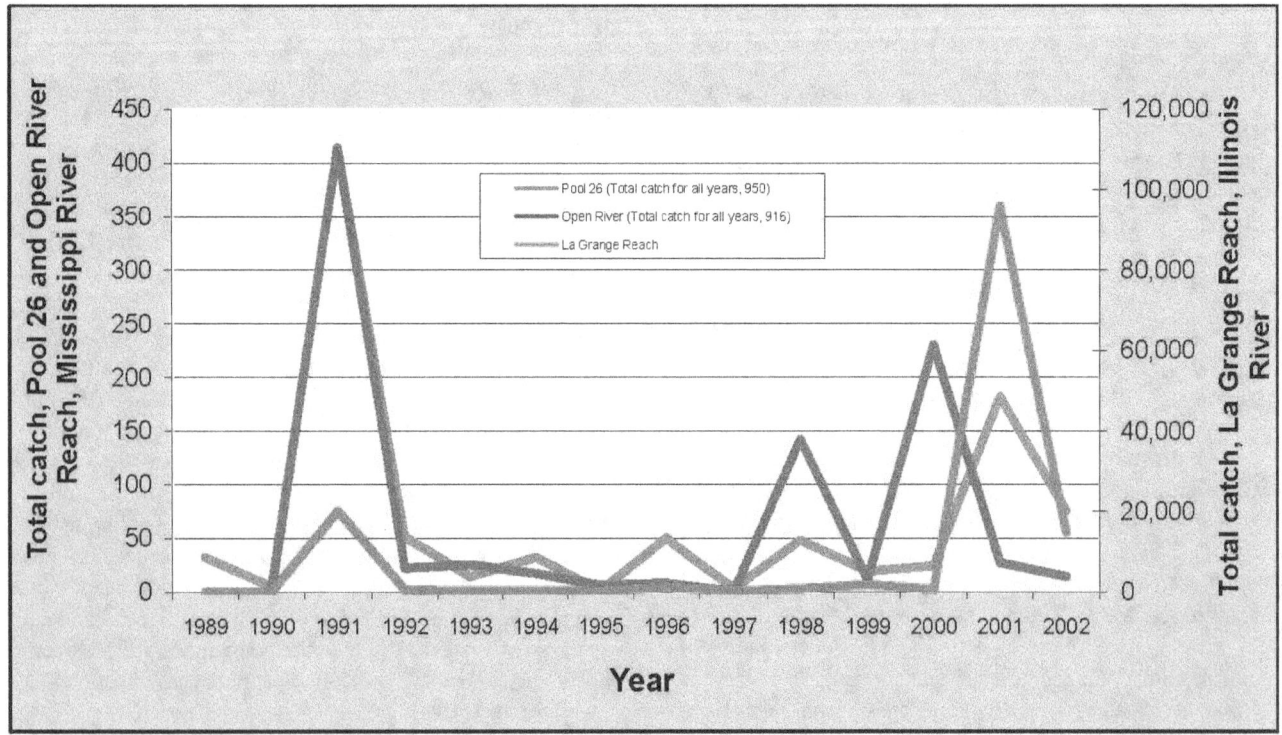

Figure 8.   Long Term Resource Monitoring Program total annual catch of threadfin shad *Dorosoma petenense* by study reach from 1989 to 2002.

Goldfish *Carassius auratus*

Native Range Biology

Goldfish are native to eastern Asia (Laird and Page, 1996). They prefer clear, vegetated pools, but can tolerate turbid waters with high concentrations of organic materials (Smith, 1979). Wild strain specimens are olivaceous or gray above, shading to yellow on lower sides. Cultured specimens can be various patterns and shades of gold, white, red, black, or orange (Smith, 1979; Pflieger, 1997). Goldfish commonly reach a length of 33 cm and can reach a maximum size of 44.7 cm (Laird and Page, 1996).

Goldfish spawning behavior is similar to that of common carp (Pflieger, 1997). Spawning begins in spring in warm shallow areas when water temperatures approach 15.6°C. Adhesive eggs are released over aquatic vegetation, tree roots, or other structures (Scott and Crossman, 1973; Laird and Page, 1996). The eggs hatch in about 3 days, depending on water temperature. Goldfish are omnivorous and feed on insects, aquatic worms, mollusks, crustaceans, and plant material (Scott and Crossman, 1973). Goldfish hybridize naturally with the common carp (Day and others, 1996; Laird and Page, 1996).

Photograph by Kevin Irons, Illinois Natural History Survey, Illinois River Biological Station

Pathway of Introduction

Goldfish appeared as pets in China as early as 960 AD, may have been introduced to Japan as early as the 1500s (Hervey and Helms, 1968; Scott and Crossman, 1973), and may have been introduced into North America as early as the late 1600s (Page and Burr, 1991). By 1889, a fish farm in Maryland was raising goldfish (Scott and Crossman, 1973). Intentional introductions in the United States into the wild may have occurred as early as the late 1600s (Courtney and Stauffer, 1990). Because of their close association with humans (as pets and as fishing bait), goldfish have been released or escaped into natural waters all over the United States from innumerable entry points (fig. 9).

Distribution in Long Term Resource Monitoring Program Study Reaches

Standardized Long Term Resource Monitoring Program monitoring indicates that goldfish are distributed throughout the lower Upper Mississippi River System drainage. Of the 465 goldfish collected by the Program, 4 were collected in the Open River Reach of the Mississippi River, 29 were collected in Pool 26 of the Mississippi River, and 432 were collected in La Grange Reach of the Illinois River. Goldfish and common carp spawn at the same time and in a similar manner, commonly resulting in hybrids (Pflieger, 1997). Of 302 common carp x goldfish hybrids collected by the Program, 15 were collected in Pool 26 of the Mississippi River, and 287 were collected in La Grange Reach of the Illinois River (fig. 10).

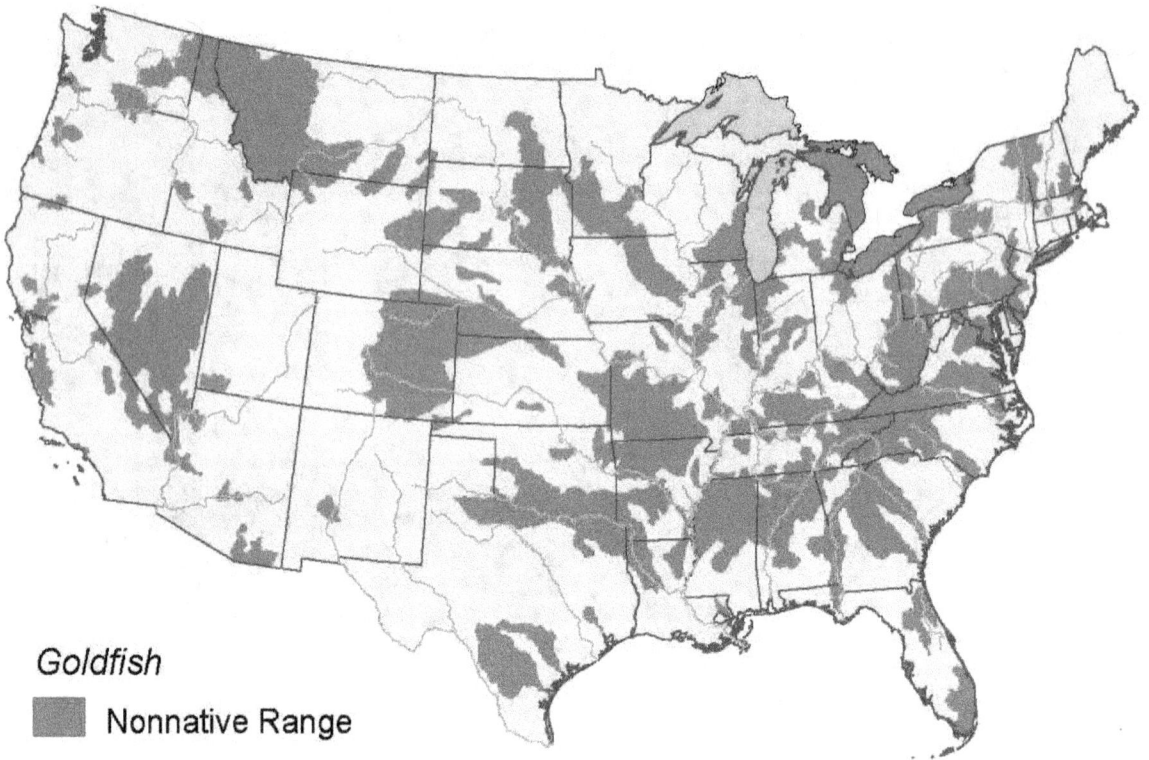

Goldfish

Nonnative Range

Figure 9. Distribution of goldfish *Carassius auratus* in the United States.

Relation of Habitat and Sampling Method to Fish Catch

Most Long Term Resource Monitoring Program goldfish collections (70.9 percent) were made in backwater contiguous-shoreline and tailwater zone habitat strata. A total of 24.1 percent of collections were made in the main channel border-unstructured and side channel border habitat strata. Eighty-nine percent of goldfish collected by the Program were caught by day and night electrofishing (76.3 percent) and fyke nets (12.7 percent; table 3)

Trends in Distribution and Abundance

Goldfish have been present in low numbers in the Long Term Resource Monitoring Program catch every year since sampling began in 1989. Although they are more numerous in some years, there is no clear trend of population increase or decrease; however, they are consistently more abundant in La Grange Reach of the Illinois River (fig. 11).

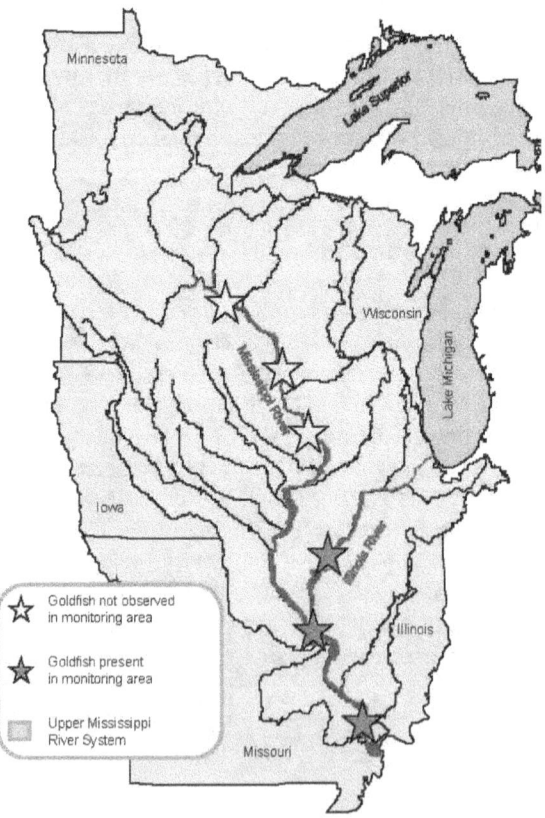

Figure 10. Long Term Resource Monitoring Program study reaches where goldfish *Carassius auratus* were collected within the Upper Mississippi River System Basin from 1989 to 2002.

Table 3. Goldfish *Carassius auratus* total catch, by strata and gear type, collected by the Long Term Resource Monitoring Program from 1989 to 2002.

[Strata abbreviations: BWC-O, backwater, contiguous-offshore; BWC-S, backwater, contiguous shoreline; IMP-O, impounded habitat-offshore; IMP-S, impounded habitat-shoreline; MCB-U, main channel border-unstructured; MCB-W, main channel border-wing dams; SCB, side channel border; TRIB, tributary mouth; TWZ, tailwater zone-400 meters below dam. Gear abbreviations: DEF, day electrofishing; F, fyke net; HL, hoop net-large; HS, hoop net-small; M, minnow fyke net; NEF, night electrofishing; S, seine; X, tandem fyke net-offshore; Y, tandem minnow fyke net-offshore. —, no catch; NA, not applicable]

		Gear									Total catch, by strata	Percentage of total catch, by strata
		DEF	F	HL	HS	M	NEF	S	X	Y		
Strata	BWC-O	—	—	1	—	—	—	—	6	1	8	1.7
	BWC-S	100	30	—	—	4	54	—	—	—	188	40.4
	IMP-O	—	—	—	—	—	—	—	2	—	2	.4
	IMP-S	4	6	—	—	—	—	—	—	—	10	2.2
	MCB-U	56	—	—	—	9	4	8	—	—	77	16.6
	MCB-W	—	—	—	—	1	—	—	—	—	1	.2
	SCB	23	—	2	—	1	4	5	—	—	35	7.5
	TRIB	1	—	1	—	—	—	—	—	—	2	0.4
	TWZ	71	23	1	7	2	38	—	—	—	142	30.5
Total catch, by gear		255	59	5	7	17	100	13	8	1	465	NA
Percentage of total catch, by gear		54.8	12.7	1.1	1.5	3.7	21.5	2.8	1.7	0.2	NA	100.0

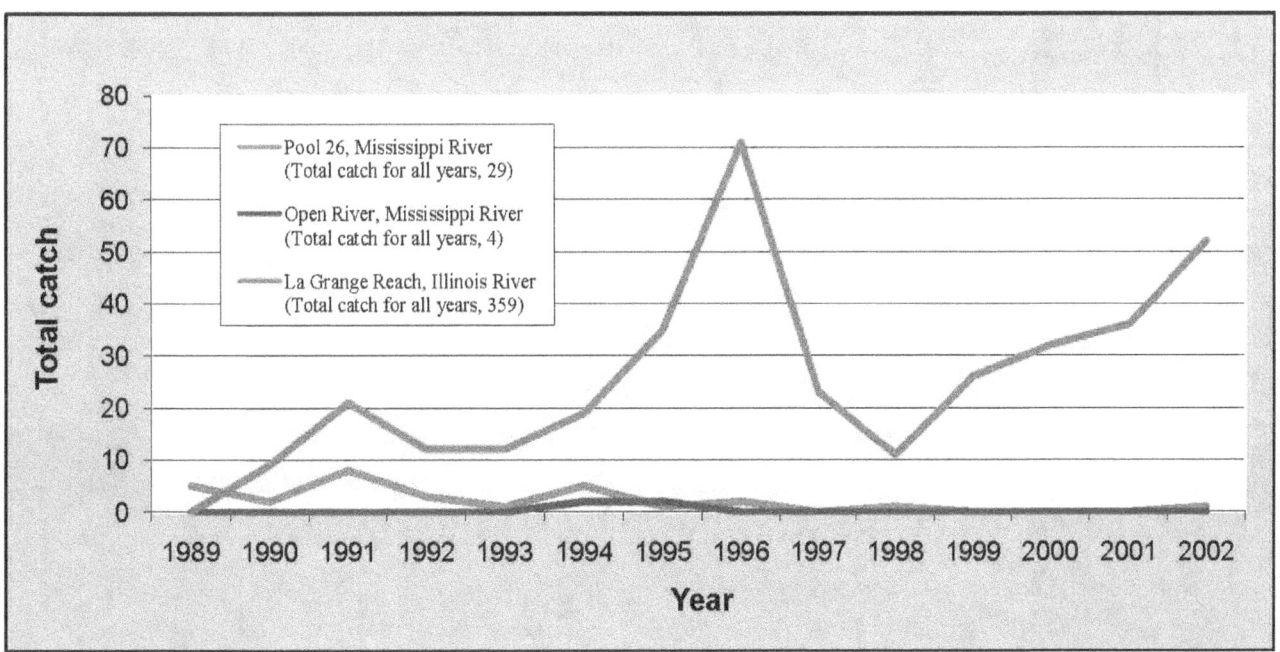

Figure 11. Long Term Resource Monitoring Program total annual catch of goldfish *Carassius auratus* by study reach from 1989 to 2002.

Ecological Impacts

Goldfish have been released at innumerable locations in the Upper Mississippi River System, but because they are not especially strong competitors with native species they have not established populations in many of the release areas. Goldfish are found in highest numbers where habitat degradation has stressed the native fish community (Smith, 1979; Laird and Page, 1996), so the likelihood that their numbers will increase in the Upper Mississippi River System is probably tied to the future ecological health of the system (Laird and Page, 1996).

Presently, goldfish probably have minimal impacts on the Upper Mississippi River System because they comprise a small portion of the fish community. However, if they become more numerous, they have the potential to compete with native species for food (McGinnis, 1984) and could indirectly affect other life-history aspects of native species (Day and others, 1996). Large numbers of goldfish could also contribute to aquatic habitat degradation in large rivers. In ponds, goldfish have been found to cause increased water turbidity (Richardson and others, 1995), much the same as common carp. Goldfish can hybridize with common carp wherever they exist together, and these hybrids actually are more abundant than either parental species in western Lake Erie (Trautman, 1981).

Discussion

Goldfish were probably the first nonnative fish species to be introduced to North America (Courtenay and others, 1984), and because of their close association with humans they have been constantly released or escaped into natural waters throughout the United States. Some states have banned the use of goldfish for fishing bait (Fuller and others, 1999), but releases into natural waters will continue because of the goldfish's status as a mainstay of the aquarium trade. Although goldfish have been taken in the wild from every state except Alaska (Courtenay and others, 1984), some of these fish probably represent recaptures of released or escaped fish rather than established populations (Lee and others, 1980). Goldfish are most successful at becoming established in areas where habitat degradation has already stressed or eliminated native fish populations (Smith, 1979; Laird and Page, 1996). Smith (1979) reported that goldfish were distributed only sporadically in Illinois, but they were common in the degraded waters of the upper Illinois River where most native fish species had been eliminated. Information from the Long Term Resource Monitoring Program indicates that goldfish populations are presently low in the Upper Mississippi River System. However, it is conceivable that populations will increase if aquatic habitats are further degraded.

Grass Carp *Ctenopharyngodon idella*

Native Range Biology

Grass carp are native to the large river systems of eastern Russia and China from the Amur River southward (Greenfield, 1973). They commonly reach a length of 76 cm and can reach a maximum size of 1.5 m in length and 32 kg in weight (Laird and Page, 1996).

Spawning of grass carp is usually triggered by rising water levels, generally in spring, but other factors such as changes in water temperature or turbidity can also trigger spawning (Stanley and others, 1978). Long stretches of flowing water are required for successful reproduction because their semibuoyant eggs (Greenfield, 1973; Laird and Page, 1996) must stay suspended in the water column by turbulence until hatching in approximately 2 days (Burr and others, 1996). After hatching, larval grass carp move to slack water areas and soon begin feeding on zooplankton and phytoplankton (Laird and Page, 1996). Grass carp can grow quickly during favorable conditions. Pflieger (1997) reported that a specimen from the Missouri River grew from 12 to 65.5 cm in only 1 year.

Grass carp are herbivorous, with large, grooved pharyngeal teeth, and a specialized intestine that allow them to shred and digest aquatic plants (Sanders and others, 1991). However, they are also reported to consume insects, worms, zooplankton, small fish, and other nonplant items, especially when young (Greenfield, 1973; Laird and Page, 1996).

Pathway of Introduction

The Bureau of Sport Fisheries and Wildlife at the Fish Farming Experimental Station, Stuttgart, Ark., introduced grass carp to the United States in 1963. The species was then stocked into other ponds and lakes in Arkansas and Alabama for vegetation control. Grass carp quickly escaped to the wild. It first appeared in the Upper Mississippi River System in 1971 in southern Illinois (Greenfield, 1973), and by 1976 it was widely distributed within the Missouri River and Upper Mississippi River System (Pflieger, 1997). Because of its popularity as a nonchemical method of vegetation control, grass carp have been widely stocked throughout the United

Photograph by Kevin Irons, Illinois Natural History Survey, Illinois River Biological Station

States (fig. 12), resulting in many entry points for grass carp to the Upper Mississippi River System. Raibley and others (1995) reported that, based on Long Term Resource Monitoring Program collections of small juveniles and some diploid (nonsterile) individuals, the grass carp was reproducing in the Illinois River and probably in the Pool 26 area of the Mississippi River. Raibley and others (1995) reported that the Long Term Resource Monitoring Program had collected a total of 61 individuals between 1990 and 1994. As of 2002, this total has grown to more than 860 individuals.

Distribution in Long Term Resource Monitoring Program Study Reaches

Although a single specimen was collected in 1994 by the Long Term Resource Monitoring Program in Pool 4 of the Mississippi River, grass carp are mainly distributed throughout the lower Upper Mississippi River System drainage basin. They are present in the Open River Reach and Pool 26 of the Mississippi River and La Grange Reach of the Illinois River (fig. 13). There is evidence of spawning and recruitment in Pool 26 of the Mississippi River and La Grange Reach of the Illinois River (Raibley and others, 1995).

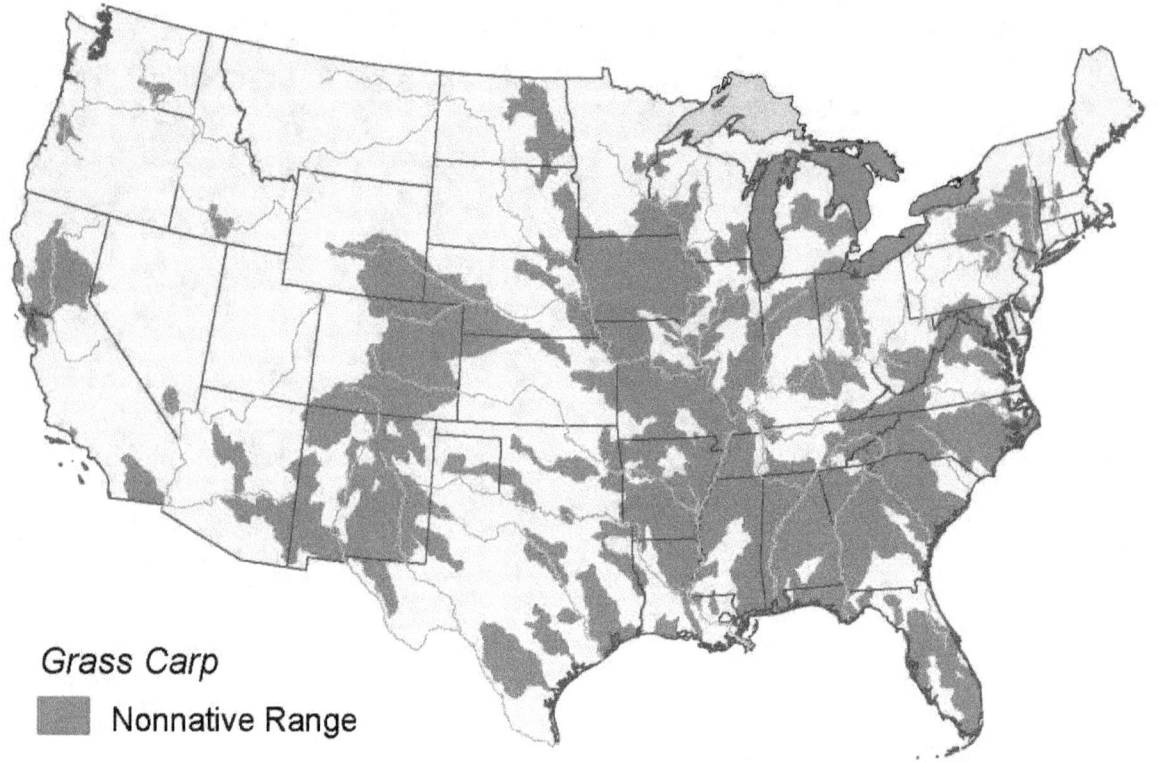

Grass Carp

▮ Nonnative Range

Figure 12. Distribution of grass carp *Ctenopharyngodon idella* in the United States.

Relation of Habitat and Sampling Method to Fish Catch

Most Long Term Resource Monitoring Program grass carp collections were made in habitat types that include shore-line areas, by use of gears that perform well near shorelines. A total of 66.6 percent of the grass carp collections were made in main channel border-unstructured and side channel border habitat types. Of the 19.6 percent of collections from back-waters, 18.1 percent came from the backwater, contiguous-shoreline, whereas only 1.5 percent came from backwater, contiguous-offshore. Day electrofishing and minnow fyke nets accounted for 70.2 percent of the grass carp catch, and seines accounted for 14.8 percent of the total catch (table 4).

Grass carp may be underrepresented in the Long Term Resource Monitoring Program catch because they are power-ful and easily startled, making them adept at avoiding capture. Oftentimes during electrofishing surveys, Pool 26 Missis-sippi River field crews will observe rustling and movement of emergent shoreline vegetation and a grass carp will dart from the vegetation, avoiding capture. In August 2002, near Missis-sippi River mile 210, field crews observed a small contiguous backwater full of grass carp feeding on flooded grasses. The grass carp were seen pulling plants (approximately 60 cm tall or taller) up by the roots and swimming to the middle of the backwater where they slowly pulled the plants underwater, presumably consuming them.

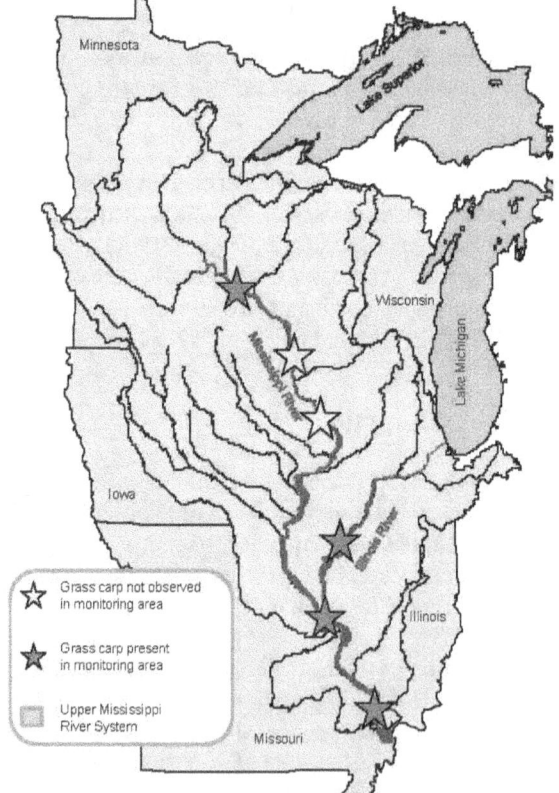

Figure 13. Long Term Resource Monitoring Program study reaches where grass carp *Ctenopharyngodon idella* were collected within the Upper Mississippi River System Basin from 1989 to 2002.

Table 4. Grass carp *Ctenopharyngodon idella* total catch, by strata and gear, collected by the Long Term Resource Monitoring Program from 1989 to 2002.

[Strata abbreviations: BWC-O, backwater, contiguous-offshore; BWC-S, backwater, contiguous-shoreline; IMP-O, impounded habitat-offshore; IMP-S, impounded habitat-shoreline; MCB-U, main channel border-unstructured; MCB-W, main channel border-wing dams; SCB, side channel border; TRIB, tributary mouth; TWZ, tailwater zone-400 meters below dam. Gear abbreviations: DEF, day electrofishing; F, fyke net; GRP, gill net-perpendicular to shore; GL, gill net-parallel to shore; HL, hoop net-large; HS, hoop net-small; M, minnow fyke net; NEF, night electrofishing; S, seine; TA, trammel net-anchored; X, tandem fyke net-offshore; Y, tandem minnow fyke net-offshore. —, no catch; NA, not applicable]

		Gear													Total catch, by strata	Percentage of total catch, by strata
		DEF	F	GRP	GL	HI	HS	M	NEF	S	TA	X	Y		
Strata	BWC-O	—	—	—	—	—	1	—	—	—	2	1	9	13	1.5
	BWC-S	79	16	—	—	—	—	41	4	15	1	—	—	156	18.1
	IMP-O	—	—	—	—	—	—	—	—	—	—	1	—	1	.1
	IMP-S	9	—	—	—	—	—	2	—	—	—	—	—	11	1.3
	MCB-U	59	—	—	—	9	5	202	—	33	—	—	—	308	35.7
	MCB-W	9	—	—	—	1	—	—	—	—	—	—	—	10	1.2
	SCB	117	—	—	8	7	—	37	18	80	—	—	—	267	30.9
	TRIB	1	—	4	—	8	1	—	—	—	—	—	—	14	1.6
	TWZ	18	3	—	—	2	—	32	28	—	—	—	—	83	9.6
Total catch, by gear		292	19	4	8	27	7	314	50	128	3	2	9	863	NA
Percentage of total catch, by gear		33.8	2.2	0.5	0.9	3.1	0.8	36.4	5.8	14.8	0.3	0.2	1.0	NA	100.0

Trends in Distribution and Abundance

Total Long Term Resource Monitoring Program catch of grass carp (fig. 14) has increased from 2 individuals from Pool 26 of the Mississippi River in 1991 to a peak of 316 individuals from Pool 26, the Open River Reach of the Mississippi River, and La Grange Reach of the Illinois River combined, in 2000. Young-of-year grass carp were not collected by the Program until 1994, when seven individuals were caught in La Grange Reach of the Illinois River. Since 1994, a total of 42 young of year have been collected in La Grange Reach of the Illinois River and 23 have been collected in Pool 26 of the Mississippi River.

Ecological Impacts

Because grass carp have voracious appetites for aquatic vegetation (Pflieger, 1997), there is concern that as grass carp populations increase, they will overgraze aquatic vegetation, negatively affecting riverine ecosystems. Removal of the wave and current dampening effects of aquatic vegetation may contribute to erosion and increase turbidity. In addition, release of nutrients previously held in plant biomass may contribute to eutrophication (Lembi and others, 1978; Chilton and Muoneke, 1992). Fish nursery areas and waterfowl feeding areas could also be reduced or eliminated (Kohler and Courtenay, 1986; Raibley and others, 1995). Fedorenko and Fraser (1978) suggest that waterfowl and some mammal populations could decline when in competition with grass carp. Yet, Chilton and Muoneke (1992) noted an increase in growth of largemouth bass after grass carp introduction. Grass carp are stocked intentionally throughout the United States to control aquatic vegetation and bolster sport fish populations. Bailey (1978) noted varying responses within several water bodies, however, the combination of effects within the aquatic environment resulting from grass carp introductions certainly can result in changes within the fish community (Cudmore and Mandrak, 2004).

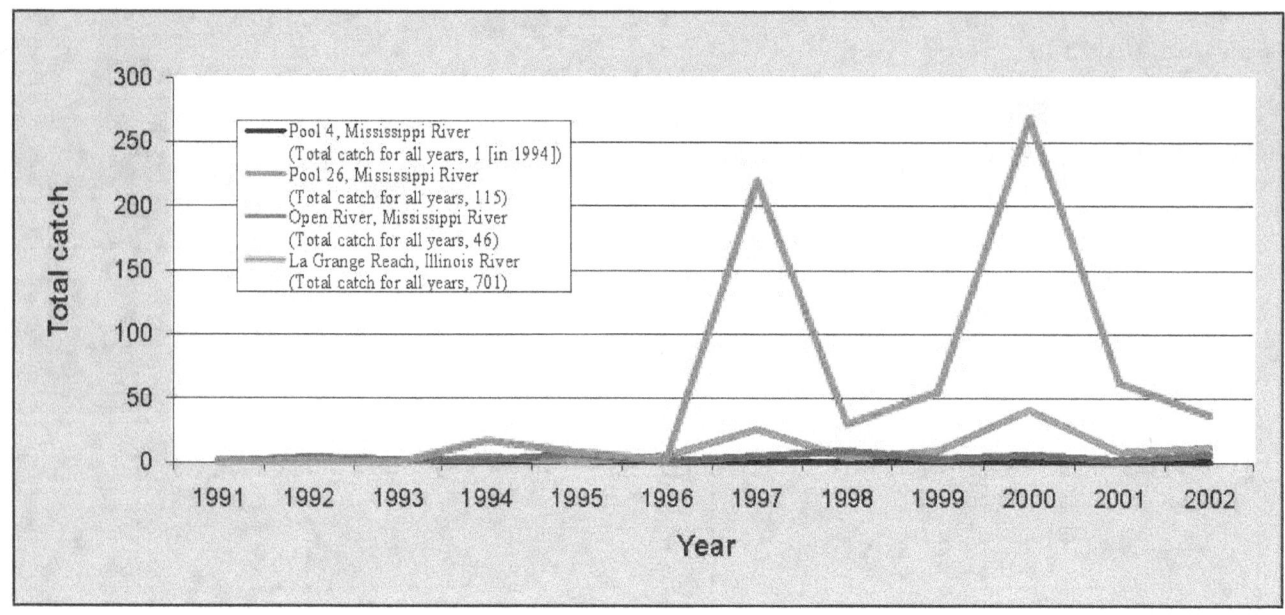

Figure 14. Long Term Resource Monitoring Program total annual catch of grass carp *Ctenopharyngodon idella* by study reach from 1989 to 2002.

Photograph by Kevin Irons, Illinois Natural History Survey, Illinois River Biological Station

Discussion

Some states have banned the stocking of grass carp altogether. Others allow the stocking of infertile triploid grass carp, whereas other states continue to allow stocking of diploid individuals (Raibley and others, 1995; Nico and Fuller, 2001). Given this inconsistent regulatory treatment of grass carp and its popularity as a biological control method for aquatic vegetation in impoundments, it is likely that grass carp will continue to spread and establish further reproducing populations in the Upper Mississippi River System.

Common Carp *Cyprinus carpio*

Native Range Biology

The common carp is native to Asia, but the full extent of its original range has been the subject of debate. Some believe that the common carp was native to parts of Europe, such as the Baltic and Caspian Sea regions (Balon, 1974; Smith, 1979), while others contend it was introduced to Europe during the Middle Ages or sooner (Forbes and Richardson, 1920; Smith, 1979; Pflieger, 1997). Common carp often exceed 77 cm in length and can reach a maximum size of 122 cm (Laird and Page, 1996).

Common carp are found in nearly all habitats, but are usually found in areas with silt or clay substrates, often near vegetation. They are omnivorous, feeding on larval and adult insects, crustaceans, mollusks, fish, worms, and plant material (Laird and Page, 1996). Common carp feed primarily on the bottom by sucking soft substrates and retaining food items. This feeding behavior often causes resuspension of bottom sediments (Bernstein and Olson, 2001). They also rise to eat suspended zooplankton or insects and plant material floating on the surface of the water (Buffler and Dickson, 1990).

Common carp begin to spawn in the northern United States and Canada in late spring and early summer (Forbes and Richardson, 1920; Scott and Crossman, 1973; Pflieger, 1997) and may continue for extended periods. Lubinski and others, (1986) reported gravid females and ripe males in Pool 19 of the Mississippi River as late as October. Common carp spawn at temperatures of 16.5 to 28.0°C, and most spawning occurs between 17 and 23°C (reviewed by Lubinski and others, 1986). Common carp spawn in warm, shallow areas. Females may contain two million or more eggs (Swee and McCrimmon, 1966) and are usually accompanied by several males during spawning. The fish do not prepare nests when they spawn; they instead broadcast the adhesive eggs during considerable splashing, which can greatly increase water turbidity. The eggs adhere to aquatic vegetation, roots, or other structure (Forbes and Richardson, 1920; Scott and Crossman, 1973; Pflieger, 1997). Eggs hatch in 3 to 6 days depending on water temperature (Swee and McCrimmon, 1966). No care is given to the eggs or fry (Pflieger, 1997).

Photograph by Illinois Natural History Survey, Great Rivers Field Station staff

Pathway of Introduction

Common carp were reportedly introduced to New York in 1831, Connecticut in the 1840s, and California in 1872, but the first successful introduction of the common carp into the United States is generally attributed to the U.S. Fish Commission (Buffler and Dixon, 1990; Fuller and others, 1999). In 1877, 345 common carp were imported by the U.S. Fish Commission and reared in ponds in the Washington, D.C., area. Approximately 12,000 young were produced and distributed to individuals in 25 states and territories to be stocked as a desirable food fish. Common carp were distributed in this manner until 1897 (Forbes and Richardson, 1920). By 1883, common carp had escaped from ponds into the Mississippi River and were reported in the Mississippi River near Hannibal, Mo., and Quincy, Ill. (Barnickol and Starrett, 1951). In 1885, common carp were intentionally stocked into major tributaries of the Mississippi River including the Illinois and Kaskaskia Rivers (Forbes and Richardson, 1920). Because of their prolific nature and ability to live in almost any type of habitat, the common carp quickly became established throughout the Upper Mississippi River System. In 1894, 205.5 metric tons of common carp were commercially harvested in the System (Buffler and Dickson, 1990).

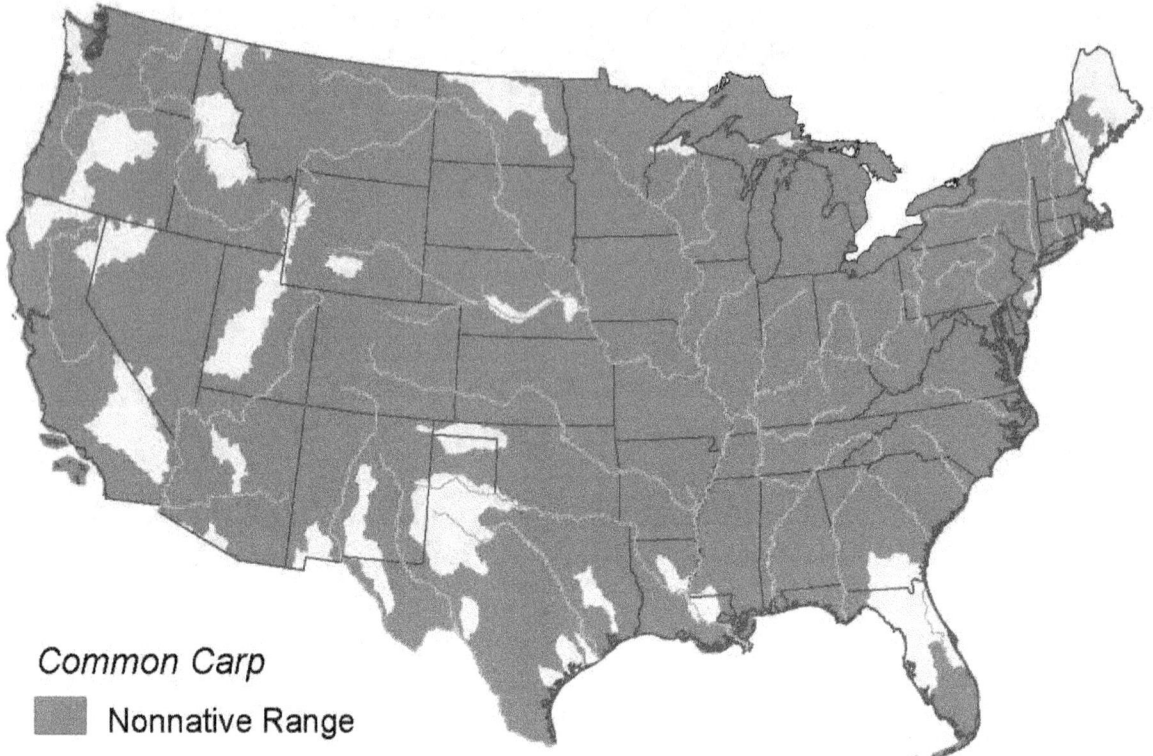

Common Carp

Nonnative Range

Figure 15. Distribution of common carp *Cyprinus carpio* in the United States.

Distribution in Long Term Resource Monitoring Program Study Reaches

Common carp have been widely distributed throughout the United States for nearly a century. They are abundant in all Long Term Resource Monitoring Program study reaches and are distributed throughout the Upper Mississippi River System drainage basin. The total common carp catch from the six study reaches from 1989 to 2002 was 135,064 individuals. Total catch by individual field stations during that period ranged from 10,447 collected in the Open River Reach of the Mississippi River to 59,175 individuals collected in La Grange Reach of the Illinois River. Common carp and goldfish spawn at the same time and in a similar manner, commonly resulting in hybrids (Pflieger. 1997). Of 302 common carp x goldfish hybrids collected by the Program, 15 were collected in Pool 26 of the Mississippi River, and 287 were collected in La Grange Reach of the Illinois River.

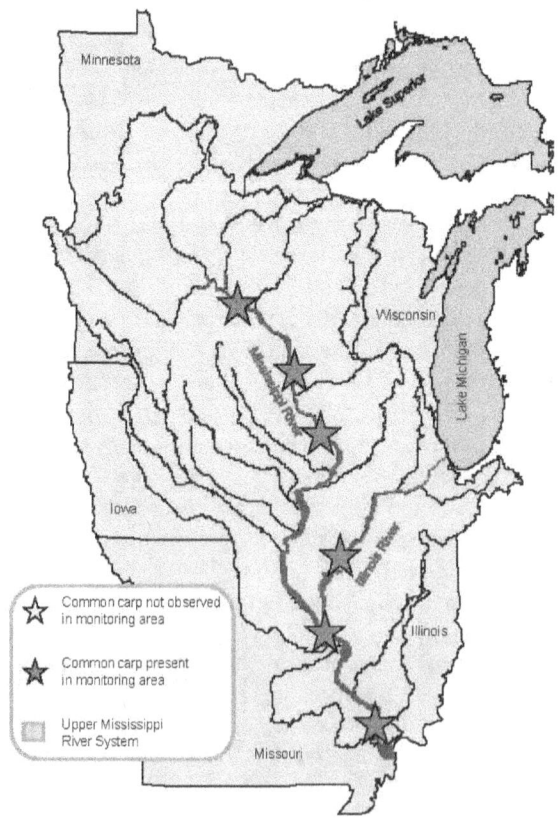

Figure 16 Long Term Resource Monitoring Program study reaches where common carp *Cyprinus carpio* were collected within the Upper Mississippi River System Basin from 1989 to 2002.

Table 5. Common carp *Cyprinus carpio* total catch, by strata and gear, collected by the Long Term Resource Monitoring Program from 1989 to 2002.

[Strata abbreviations: BWC-O, backwater, contiguous-offshore; BWC-S, backwater, contiguous-shoreline; IMP-O, impounded habitat-offshore; IMP-S, impounded habitat-shoreline; MCB-U, main channel border-unstructured; MCB-W, main channel border-wing dams; SCB, side channel border; TRIB, tributary mouth; TWZ, tailwater zone-400 meters below dam. Gear abbreviations: DEF, day electrofishing; F, fyke net; G, gill net; HL, hoop net-large; HS, hoop net-small; H, hoop net-bridled large and small; M, minnow fyke net; NEF, night electrofishing; S, seine; T, trawl; TA, trammel net-anchored; X, tandem fyke net-offshore; Y, tandem minnow fyke net-offshore. —, no catch]

		Gear														Total catch, by strata	Percent-age of total catch, by strata
		DEF	F	G	HL	HS	H	M	NEF	S	T	TA	X	Y		
Strata	BWC-O	121	—	510	1,086	591	—	—	6	—	—	259	1,804	1,497	5,874	4.3
	BWC-S	15,943	5,464	46	—	—	—	1,768	2,636	471	—	120	69	1	26,518	19.6
	IMP-O	47	18	22	980	559	15	235	27	—	—	33	309	165	2,410	1.8
	IMP-S	2,087	1,180	—	—	—	—	1,821	—	381	—	—	—	—	5,469	4.0
	MCB-U	10,734	68	38	5,500	3,355	2,462	2,517	2,080	2,383	58	—	—	—	29,195	21.6
	MCB-W	2,885	87	2	656	506	205	126	412	—	—	—	—	—	4,879	3.6
	SCB	18,368	160	176	6,888	2,914	2,563	1,322	6,269	277	—	—	—	—	38,937	28.8
	TRIB	636	165	124	1,034	671	21	66	19	—	—	—	—	—	2,736	2.0
	TWZ	2,756	691	—	3,401	2,368	1,826	185	7,796	10	99	—	—	—	19,132	14.2
Total catch, by gear		53,577	7,833	918	19,545	10,964	7,092	8,040	19,245	3,522	157	412	2,182	1,663	135,150	—
Percentage of total catch, by gear		39.6	5.8	0.7	14.5	8.1	5.2	5.9	14.2	2.6	0.1	0.3	1.6	1.2		100.0

Relation of Habitat and Sampling Method to Fish Catch

Most Long Term Resource Monitoring Program collections of common carp (fig. 16) (70.0 percent) were made in main channel border-unstructured, side channel border, and backwater, contiguous-shoreline habitat strata. Common carp were caught in all sampling gears used by the Program. Day electrofishing accounted for 39.6 percent of common carp collected, large hoop nets accounted for 14.5 percent, and night electrofishing accounted for 14.2 percent of the total catch (table 5).

Trends in Distribution and Abundance

Abundance within Long Term Resource Monitoring Program catches indicates that common carp populations increased through the mid-1990s (fig. 17). The year of the "Great Flood" (1993) was an exception, because catches were much lower than expected. High water, which dilutes catches and scatters fish, along with decreased sampling effort because of the high water in 1993, are probable causes for this decreased catch. Between 1994 and 1996, catches reached a peak and began a decline in all of the study reaches except Pool 4 and the Open River of the Mississippi River, where populations remained relatively stable.

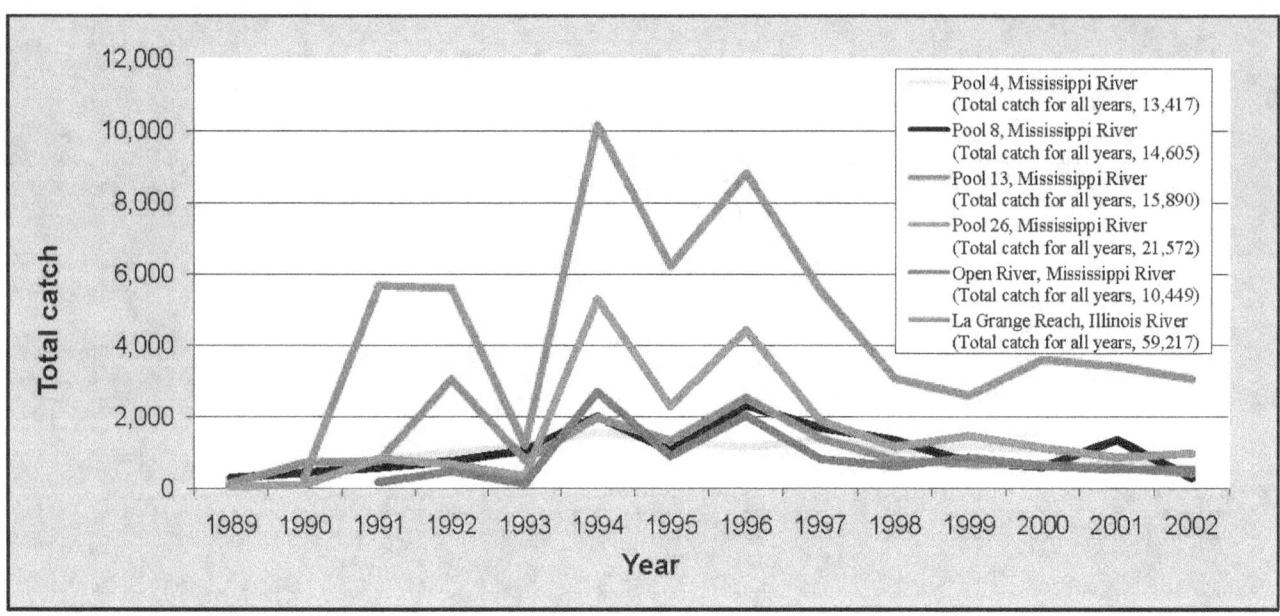

Figure 17.   Long Term Resource Monitoring Program total annual catch of common carp *Cyprinus carpio* by study reach from 1989 to 2002.

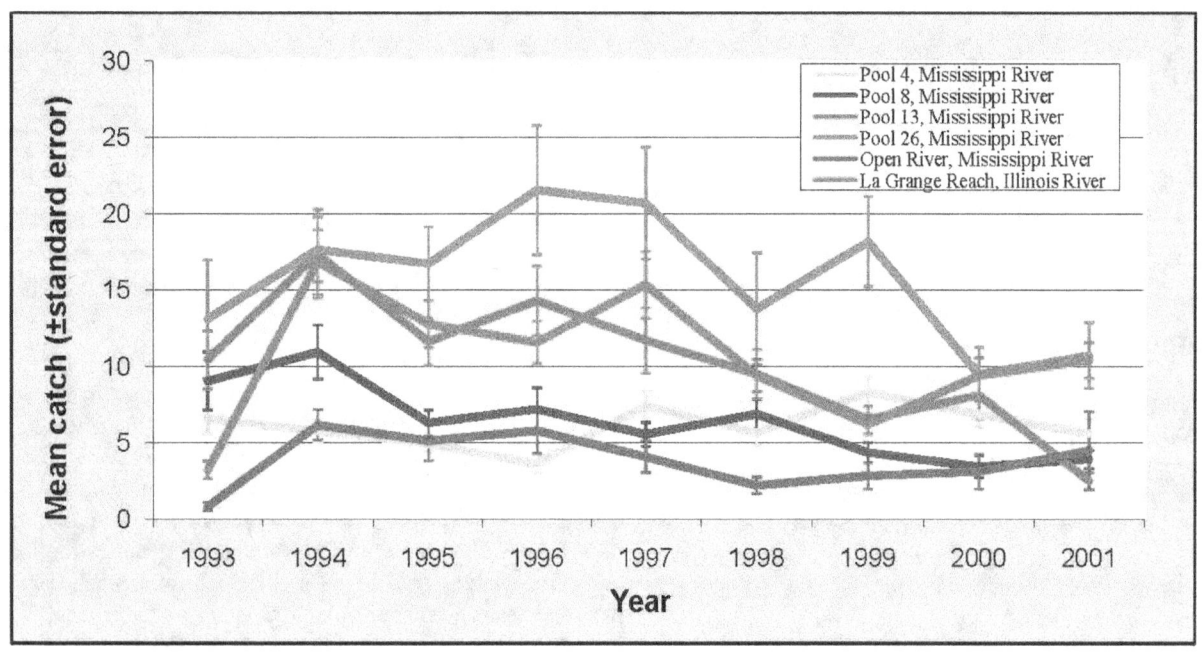

Figure 18.   Mean number of common carp *Cyprinus carpio* collected per electrofishing run by year from all Long Term Resource Monitoring Program reaches, 1993–2001.

Ecological Impacts

Common carp are often blamed for increases in turbidity, declines in submersed aquatic vegetation, and other impacts. Attribution of these impacts to common carp in the Upper Mississippi River System, however, is confounded by its simultaneous spread with urbanization, industrialization, and conversion of much of the watershed to agriculture. The resulting increases in sewage, industrial waste, and turbidity may have given common carp a competitive advantage over native species that were less tolerant of poor water quality (Berstein and Olson, 2001).

Declines in game fish populations are often seen after common carp invade watersheds, although effects can be confounded by land use changes. Common carp can be destructive to the vegetated and clear water habitat required by many native fishes and may compete with ecologically similar species, such as carpsuckers and buffalos (Summerfelt and others, 1970; Laird and Page, 1996). Subsequent declines in game fish populations are often seen as common carp become established. Common carp may also be detrimental to native fishes simply because their density can be so high in a small area, such as an isolated backwater, that they may interfere with territorial nest-building species such as Centrarchids (Lubinski and others, 1986). The feeding and spawning behavior of common carp causes several water-quality problems including increased nutrient recycling, turbidity, and reduced macrophyte growth (Berstein and Olson, 2001).

Discussion

Because the common carp was ubiquitous in the Upper Mississippi River System before many of the first fish surveys were conducted, its impacts on some native species are difficult to ascertain. However, negative impacts of common carp on game fish and ecologically similar species have been documented, as well as its negative impact on water quality and macrophytes.

Since their establishment in the 1880s, common carp have gone in and out of favor as a food fish (Buffler and Dickson, 1990), but have remained a substantial component of the commercial fish harvest on the Mississippi River. For example, of more than 20 species of fish harvested by Illinois commercial fishermen in the Mississippi River Pools 12 through 26 in 2001, common carp were the second most harvested species with a total of 264,267 kg reported with an estimated value of $52, 435 (Maher, 2002).

Common carp have been a part of the Upper Mississippi River System fish fauna for more than 100 years. Because common carp can tolerate poor water quality and can use a wide variety of habitats and food sources, they will probably continue to be a dominant part of the Upper Mississippi River System fish community (Lubinski and others, 1986). Common carp were the fourth most abundant fish in Long Term Resource Monitoring Program collections from 1993 to 2002.

Photograph by Chad Dolan, Illinois Natural History Survey, Great Rivers Field Station

Silver Carp *Hypophthalmichthys molitrix*

Photograph by David Riecks, University of Illinois

Native Range Biology

Silver carp are native to large lakes and rivers of southern Asia, eastern China, and Siberia, ranging from 21°N to 64°N latitude (Laird and Page, 1996; Xie and Chen, 2001; Froese and Pauly, 2004).

In their native range, silver carp migrate seasonally between river and connected lakes. They spawn during the monsoon season when water temperatures are from 18.3 to 23.5°C (Verigin and others, 1978; Xie and Chen, 2001). Silver carp spawning habits are similar to those of bighead and grass carp. Their eggs are semibuoyant and travel with water, often moving at velocities from 0.78 to 2.26 m/s (Chang, 1966; Jennings, 1988; Robison and Buchanan, 1988; Laird and Page 1996). Fry hatch in approximately 1 day and float with the larval drift, where after 7 days they migrate toward shore (Jennings, 1988; Etnier and Starnes, 1993). Silver carp can mature in 3 to 6 years and have a maximum size greater than 1,000 mm and 27.3 kg (Kamilov and Salikhov, 1996; Laird and Page, 1996). Silver carp are filter feeders, consuming phytoplankton, zooplankton, and other food stuffs as small as 3.2 µm by entrapment of food in the mucus of their gill rakers, and they physically filter food stuffs as small as 10 µm (Omarov, 1970; Kucklentz, 1985; Herodek and others, 1989; Smith, 1989; De-Shang and Shuang-Lin, 1996; Vörös, 1997). Silver carp can travel in large schools and generally swim just below the surface (Kamilov and Salikhov, 1996).

Pathway of Introduction

Silver carp were brought into Arkansas for aquaculture purposes in 1973 (Henderson, 1976; Tucker and others, 1996). Most likely, the fish escaped aquaculture facilities in central Lonoke County, Ark., and spread into Arkansas rivers and streams. In fall 1981, silver carp were limited to the Arkansas and White River systems. Some combination of natural reproduction and escape has aided the spreading of the species into the lower Mississippi River and subsequent expansion into the Upper Mississippi River System (fig. 19) (Freeze and Henderson, 1982).

Silver carp were first collected in Upper Mississippi River System waters as early as 1983, evidenced by a silver carp at a commercial market in Jackson County, Ill., approximately Mississippi River mile 80 (Illinois Natural History Survey fish collections, written commun., 2003). Additional silver carp were documented in the Mississippi River below Lock and Dam 19 in 1986 at river mile 363 (Illinois Natural History Survey fish collections), 1996 at river mile 160 (Burr and others, 1996), and 2000 (Long Term Resource Monitoring Program, written commun., 2001). At present, silver carp are expanding quite rapidly within the river system. An electronic barrier in Romeoville, Ill., originally designed to limit expansion of the round goby range, has gained support because it is believed that it will stop bighead and silver carp from expanding quickly into the Great Lakes Basin (Stokstad, 2003).

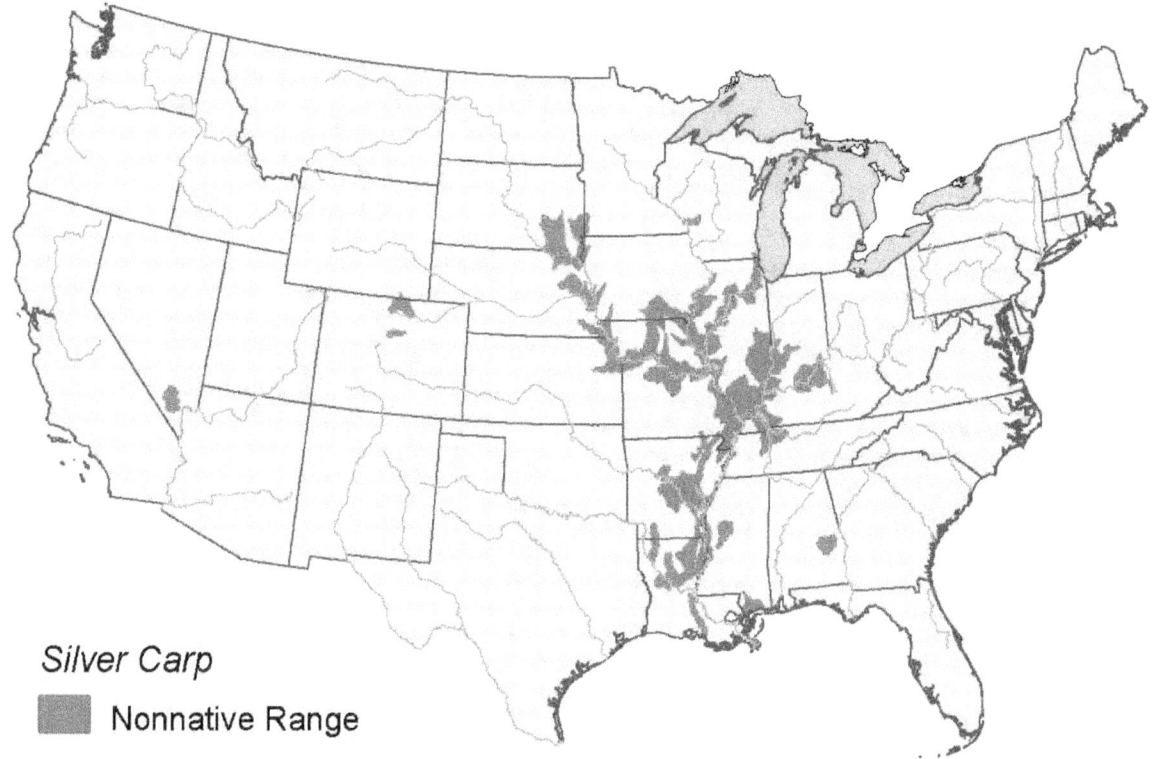

Silver Carp

Nonnative Range

Figure 19. Distribution of silver carp *Hypophthalmichthys molitrix* in the United States.

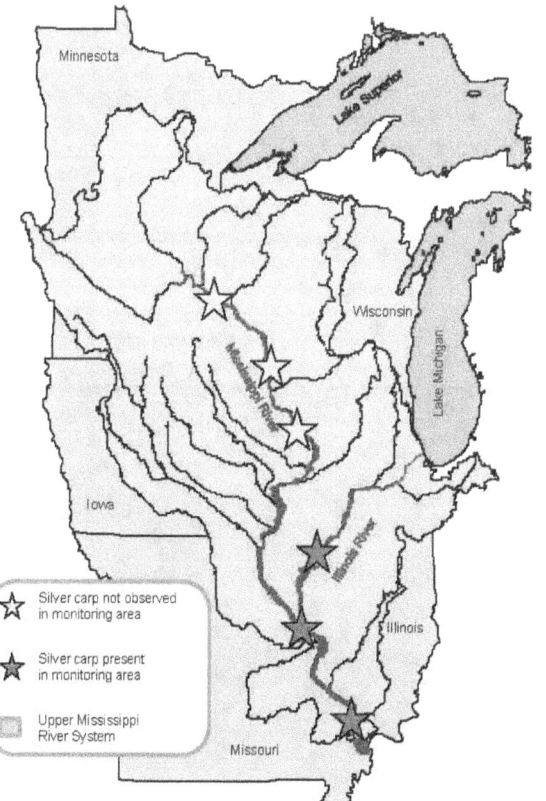

Silver carp not observed in monitoring area

Silver carp present in monitoring area

Upper Mississippi River System

Figure 20. Long Term Resource Monitoring Program study reaches where silver carp *Hypophthalmichthys molitrix* were collected within the Upper Mississippi River System Basin from 1989 to 2002.

Distribution in Long Term Resource Monitoring Program Study Reaches

Silver carp are found in three of the six Long Term Resource Monitoring Program study reaches, the Open River Reach and Pool 26 of the Mississippi River, and La Grange Reach of the Illinois River (fig. 20). Silver carp were first collected in Program study reaches in 1998. Four individuals were collected in electrofishing samples in Pool 26 of the Mississippi River (two fish) and La Grange Reach of the Illinois River (two fish). Field crews from the Open River Reach of the Mississippi River first caught silver carp in multiple gears in 2000. Focused research by the Program also documented silver carp in Pool 20 of the Mississippi River, in fall 2000. To date, the Program has not collected silver carp in or above Pool 13 of the Mississippi River.

Relation of Habitat and Sampling Method to Fish Catch

Silver carp were first collected by the Long Term Resource Monitoring Program in 1998 by electrofishing. Two fish were collected in Pool 26 of the Mississippi River in side channel border habitat by electrofishing and two fish were collected in La Grange Reach of the Illinois River in main channel border habitat by electrofishing. Side channel border habitats account for 56.9 percent of the silver carp collected since 1998. Furthermore, 19.0 percent of the silver carp were collected from backwater habitats (shoreline and offshore combined). Main channel border unstructured habitat accounted for 11.5 percent, and collections around wing dams in the main channel border accounted for 0.7 percent of the total catch. The tailwater zone, a small 200- to 400-m stretch of habitat below lock and dams, accounts for 8.5 percent of the total silver carp caught by Long Term Resource Monitoring Program. Although 2.7 percent of silver carp were collected from tributary mouth habitat, only the Program's Open River Reach Field Station collects these data in this habitat. However, ancillary field observations have confirmed that silver carp are using tributaries and their mouths in La Grange Reach of the Illinois River year round.

Day electrofishing accounted for 62.0 percent of the silver carp collected from all Long Term Resource Monitoring Program collections. Night electrofishing (9.5 percent), minnow fyke net (92 percent), and seines (7.5 percent) combined with day electrofishing accounted for more than 88 percent of all silver carp collected. Silver carp are susceptible to gill and trammel nets; however, these gear types are not standard within Program protocols and, thus, are infrequently deployed. Minnow fyke nets rarely catch silver carp older than young of year; therefore, this gear type is valuable in determining year-class strength (Long Term Resource Monitoring Program written commun., 2002; table 6).

Silver carp have been found to have high localized high densities in certain habitat types, especially in side channel and main channel border that provides refuge from current (inside bends; field observations–La Grange Reach of the Illinois River; Freeze and Henderson ,1982). In addition, Illinois Natural History Survey personnel have observed large schools of silver carp swimming away from boats and eluding electrofishing surveys.

Table 6. Silver carp *Hypophthalmichthys molitrix* total catch, by strata and gear, collected by the Long Term Resource Monitoring Program from 1989 to 2002.

[Strata abbreviations: BWC-O, backwater, contiguous-offshore; BWC-S, backwater, contiguous-shoreline; IMP-O, impounded habitat-offshore; IMP-S, impounded habitat-shoreline; MCB-U, main channel border-unstructured; MCB-W, main channel border-wing dams; SCB, side channel border; TRIB, tributary mouth; TWZ, tailwater zone-400 meters below dam. Gear abbreviations: DEF, day electrofishing; F, fyke net; GR, gill net-perpendicular to shore; GL, gill net-parallel to shore; HL, hoop net-large; HS, hoop net-small; M, minnow fyke net; NEF, night electrofishing; S, seine; TA, trammel net-anchored; X, tandem fyke net-offshore; Y, tandem minnow fyke net-offshore. —, no catch; NA, not applicable]

							Gear								
		DEF	F	GR	GL	HI	HS	M	NEF	S	TA	X	Y	Total catch, by strata	Percentage of total catch, by strata
Strata	BWC-O	0	—	—	—	2	—	—	—	—	—	7	2	11	3.7
	BWC-S	44	—	—	—	—	—	1	—	—	—	—	—	45	15.3
	IMP-O	—	—	—	—	3	—	—	—	—	1	—	—	4	1.4
	MCB-U	16	—	—	—	—	—	14	—	2	—	—	—	32	10.8
	MCB-W	2	—	—	—	—	—	—	—	—	—	—	—	2	.7
	SCB	104	—	—	8	5	—	12	19	20	—	—	—	168	56.9
	TRIB	4	—	2	—	1	1	—	—	—	—	—	—	8	2.7
	TWZ	13	3	—	—	—	—	—	9	—	—	—	—	25	8.5
Total catch, by gear		183	3	2	8	11	1	27	28	22	1	7	2	295	NA
Percentage of total catch, by gear		62.0	1.0	0.7	2.7	3.7	0.3	9.2	9.5	7.5	0.3	2.4	0.7	NA	100.0

Trends in Distribution and Abundance

The total number of silver carp collected by the Long Term Resource Monitoring Program has increased from four individuals in Pool 26 of the Mississippi River and La Grange Reach of the Illinois River in 1998 to a high of 114 individuals from the Open River Reach and Pool 26 of the Mississippi River, and La Grange Reach of the Illinois River combined in 2000 (fig. 21).

Silver carp catches were highest in 2000 due to high reproductive success in 2000, and many young-of-year individuals were collected in all three Program reaches where they occurred (Long Term Resource Monitoring Program written commun., 2002; Chick and Pegg, 2001). The 2000 silver carp year class began to mature in 2003. Thus, the population is established and reproduction will further the silver carp's invasion, bolstering the population within the Upper Mississippi River System.

Ecological and Economic Impacts

Silver carp are large planktivorious filter feeders that have the ability to impact all fish species in the Upper Mississippi River System because their feeding habits are similar to those of the larval and juvenile fish of other species within like habitats (Benson and others, 2001). In addition, silver carp may compete with other native filter feeders of the river

system such as paddlefish, gizzard shad, various minnow species, and buffalo fish (*Ictiobus* spp.; Chick and Pegg, 2001). Silver carp can directly impact the economy if they suppress paddlefish and buffalo fisheries in the Upper Mississippi River System and a market for silver carp does not develop. The commercial value of paddlefish and buffalo in the Illinois River in 2001 was $131,500 (Maher, 2002). As of 2001, bighead and silver carp accounted for 2.4 percent of the estimated value of the commercial fishery in Illinois (all waters) with a total of 140,385 kg or 5 percent of the total commercial harvest by weight in Illinois (Maher, 2002). Because silver carp have been introduced throughout the world, evidence exists that these introductions have led to decreased species diversity and abundance in commercial catches (Spaturu and Gophen, 1985; Sugunan, 1997; Petr, 2002).

Local and national journalists have documented many reports of people hit by large jumping silver carp after the passing of a boat or a loud noise. These strikes have occurred within the lower Upper Mississippi River System. It is not hard to imagine that a collision between a passenger on a boat and an airborne silver carp could be quite painful, and it puts a passenger at risk of physical injury or being knocked from a boat. Researchers erect fencing on their vessels and crappie anglers carry trash can lids or folding chairs to deflect jumping fish (fig. 22). As these incidents increase, economic impacts on recreation and tourism are possible in the form of lost expenditures related to venue changes and in costs associated with medical treatment.

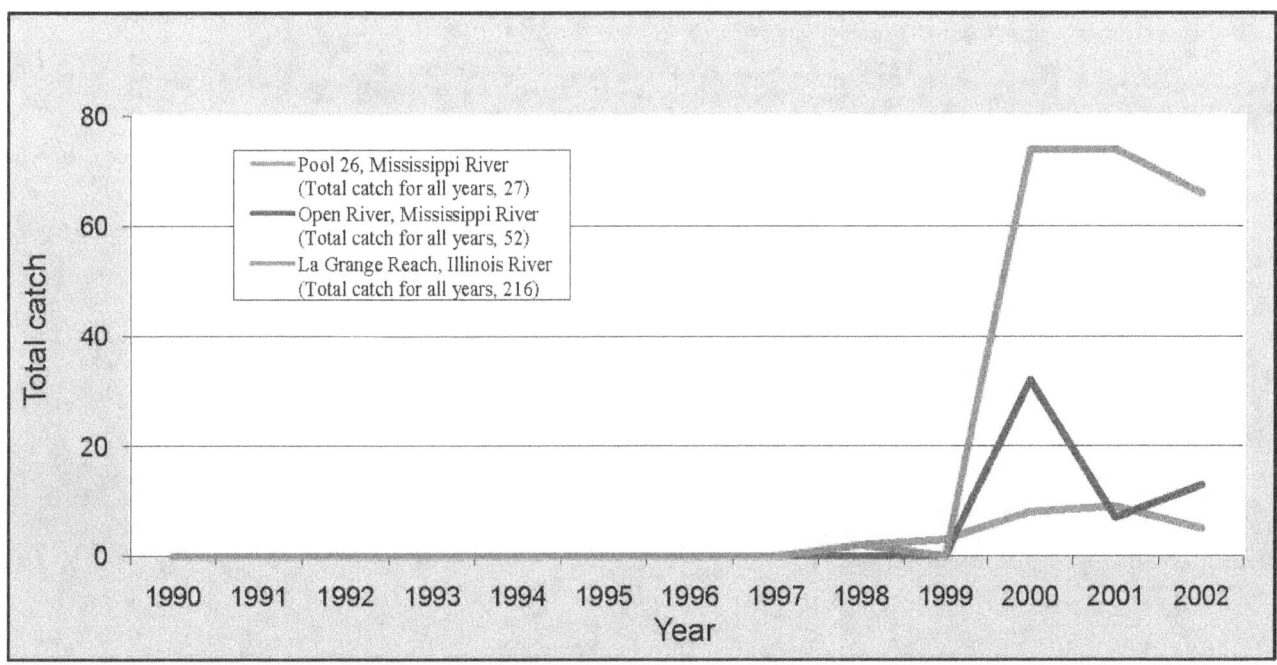

Figure 21.   Long Term Resource Monitoring Program total annual catch of silver carp *Hypophthalmichthys molitrix* by study reach from 1989 to 2002.

Discussion

Native distributions in China and naturalized populations elsewhere in Asia suggest that the silver carp may be able to establish populations in much of the Upper Mississippi River System Basin as well as expand into Canada. Silver carp have been introduced into at least 90 countries, mostly for aquaculture and biological control of algae (Kolar and others, 2007). The likelihood of this species competing with other filter feeders, as well as the plankton-dependent young of year of many native fishes, is high. Locally high abundances of silver carp in side channels and tributaries, as observed in La Grange Reach of the Illinois River, suggest that this species will probably affect other fish species and energy flow through the Upper Mississippi River System food web. Silver carp is the most intensively cultured freshwater fish species in the world. It is likely that this fish would have potential as a food fish marketed whole or canned and could potentially be competitive with the tuna market, as bighead carp studies have shown (Food and Agriculture Organization of the United Nations, 1999; Stone and others, 2000). Young-of-year and juvenile silver carp, and to some degree bighead carp, look similar to gizzard shad and threadfin shad and are often collected together to be used as bait. Asian carp could be introduced in other waters if they are misidentified, and, for this reason, it is now illegal to collect bait from below Gavins Point Dam in South Dakota (South Dakota 2004 Fishing Regulations, 2004).

Figure 22.   Silver carp jumping due to the passing of a boat on the Illinois River, Havana, Ill. (Photograph by Rick Wood, Milwaukee Journal Sentinel)

Bighead Carp *Hypophthalmichthys nobilis*

Native Range Biology

Bighead carp are native to large lakes and rivers in eastern Asia, ranging from the Pearl River in South China (17°N latitude) to the Yellow River in North China (36°N latitude; Laird and Page, 1996; Xie and Chen, 2001). However, bighead carp populations have become established in other, more northern rivers in Asia, demonstrating the potential for their distribution through Pool 1 of the Mississippi River to approximately river mile 856 (Jennings, 1988).

In their native range, bighead carp migrate seasonally between rivers and connected lakes. They spawn during the monsoon season when water temperatures are from 18.3 to 23.5°C (Verigin and others, 1978; Xie and Chen, 2001). Bighead carp eggs are semibuoyant and travel with water, often moving at velocities from 0.78 to 2.26 m/s (Chang, 1966; Jennings, 1988; Laird and Page, 1996). Fry hatch in about 1 day and drift with the current until approximately 7 days posthatch, and then they migrate toward shore (Jennings, 1988; Etnier and Starnes, 1993). Bighead carp mature as early as 2 years old and have a maximum size greater than 1.5 m in length and 40 kg in weight (Jennings, 1988; Laird and Page, 1996). Bighead carp are filter feeders that consume phytoplankton and zooplankton. In addition, Lazareva and others, (1977) found that in pond experiments where food may have been limiting, detritus dominated the diets of 1- and 2-year-old bighead carp.

Pathway of Introduction

Bighead carp were first brought to Arkansas for aquaculture purposes in the early 1970s (Henderson, 1976; Jennings, 1988; Tucker and others, 1996; Stone, 2000; Rasmussen, 2002). It is likely that bighead carp escaped aquaculture facilities and established populations in rivers and streams in the southern United States. Bighead carp were first collected in the Ohio River at river mile 919 in 1981, the Middle Illinois River at river mile 99 in 1986, and then the Upper Mississippi River at river mile 364 in Pool 20 in 1986 and at approximately river mile 413 in Pool 18 in 1987 (Jennings, 1988; Rasmussen, 2002). Prolific natural reproduction and possible further escapes have enabled the bighead carp to spread and to become firmly established within the Upper Mississippi River System since its initial introduction (Long Term Resource Monitoring Program, written commun., 2002).

Photograph by David Riecks, University of Illinois

Figure 23. Raising trammel nets with bighead carp *Hypophthalmichthys nobilis* in Pool 26, Mississippi River. (Photograph by Eric Gittinger, Illinois Natural History Survey, Great Rivers Field Station, 2000)

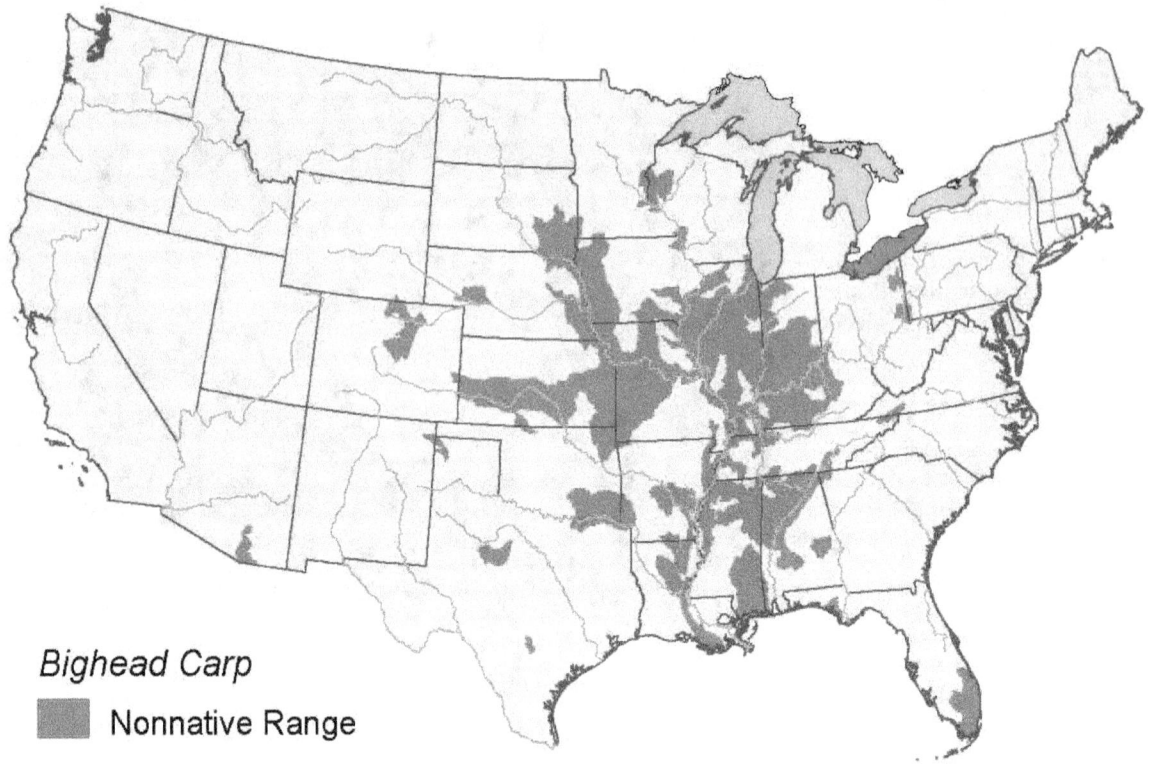

Bighead Carp

Nonnative Range

Figure 24.   Distribution of bighead carp *Hypophthalmichthys nobilis* in the United States.

Most recently, bighead carp have been found in the Des Moines River, a tributary of the Mississippi River (U.S. Geological Survey, 2004). On the edge of expansion within the Mississippi River, anecdotal reports from commercial fishermen include catches in the Iowa River below Iowa City, Iowa; 1.8–3.2 kg bighead carp totaling more than 90 kg in Pool 18 of the Mississippi River; and large bighead carp ranging from 11 to 18 kg from Pool 17 of the Mississippi River (1998 to present, Mel Bowler, Iowa Department of Natural Resources/Long Term Resource Monitoring Program, Bellevue, Iowa, oral commun., 2003). Bighead carp are expanding quite rapidly within the Upper Mississippi River System. A proposed electronic barrier in Romeoville, Ill., that originally was designed to limit expansion of the round goby range has gained support because it is believed that it will stop bighead and silver carp from expanding quickly into the Great Lakes Basin (Stokstad, 2003).

Distribution in Long Term Resource Monitoring Program Study Reaches

Bighead carp have been found in three of the six Long Term Resource Monitoring Program study reaches, the Open River Reach and Pool 26 of the Mississippi River and La Grange Reach of the Illinois River (fig. 25). The Program first collected bighead carp in 1991, when one individual was

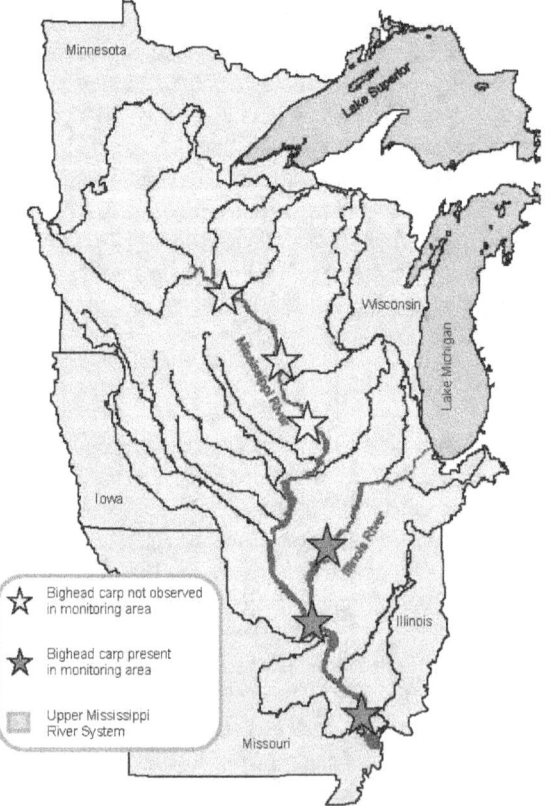

Figure 25.   Long Term Resource Monitoring Program study reaches where bighead carp *Hypophthalmichthys nobilis* were collected (red stars) within the Upper Mississippi River System Basin from 1989 to 2002.

collected in Pool 26 of the Mississippi River. Subsequent Program collections documented the spread of bighead carp throughout the Upper Mississippi River System; they were found in the Open River Reach in 1992 and in La Grange Reach of the Illinois River in 1995. To date, the Long Term Resource Monitoring Program has not collected bighead carp in or above Pool 13 of the Mississippi River.

Relation of Habitat and Sampling Method to Fish Catch

Bighead carp were first collected by the Long Term Resource Monitoring Program near a wing dam off the main channel in Pool 26 of the Mississippi River; however, only 23 individuals have been collected in this habitat as of 2002. More than 50 percent of the bighead carp collected by the Program have come from either side channel border or tailwater zone habitat strata. Furthermore, nearly 24 percent of the bighead carp have been collected from backwater, contiguous-shoreline and backwater, contiguous-offshore habitat strata combined. The main channel border-unstructured habitat has accounted for 17.6 percent of the total catch, whereas main channel border-wing dam habitat has accounted for only 0.9

percent. Although 5.0 percent of bighead carp were collected from tributary habitat, only the Program's Open River Reach Field Station collects data in this habitat. However, ancillary field observations have confirmed that bighead carp are using this habitat (tributaries and their mouths) in La Grange Reach year round.

From all Long Term Resource Monitoring Program collections, minnow fyke nets accounted for 32.3 percent of bighead carp total catch and large hoop nets accounted for 26.7 percent. Minnow fyke nets catch almost exclusively young-of-year bighead carp; therefore, the gear is valuable for determining year-class strength (Long Term Resource Monitoring Program, written commun., 2002). Larger, subadult and adult bighead carp were collected by use of large hoop nets (26.7 percent of the catch), day electrofishing (10.5 percent of the catch) and fyke nets (9.8 percent of the catch; table 7).

Bighead carp frequently exhibit high local densities, especially in side channel and main channel border habitat that provides refuge from current, including inside bends (Long Term Resource Monitoring Program, written commun., 2002; Freeze and Henderson, 1982). In addition, Illinois Natural History Survey personnel have observed large schools of bighead carp swimming away from boats and eluding electrofishing surveys.

Table 7. Bighead carp *Hypophthalmichthys nobilis* total catch, by strata and gear, collected by the Long Term Resource Monitoring Program from 1989 to 2002.

[Strata abbreviations: BWC-O, backwater, contiguous-offshore; BWC-S, backwater, contiguous-shoreline; IMP-O, impounded habitat-offshore; IMP-S, impounded habitat-shoreline; MCB-U, main channel border-unstructured; MCB-W, main channel border-wing dams; SCB, side channel border; TRIB, tributary mouth; TWZ, tailwater zone-400 meters below dam. Gear abbreviations: DEF, day electrofishing; F, fyke net; GL, gill net-parallel to shore; HL, hoop net-large; HS, hoop net-small; M, minnow fyke net; NEF, night electrofishing; S, seine; TA, trammel net-anchored; X, tandem fyke net-offshore; Y, tandem minnow fyke net-offshore. —, no catch; NA, not applicable]

| | | Gear | | | | | | | | | | | Total catch, by strata | Percentage of total catch, by strata |
		DEF	F	GL	HL	HS	M	NEF	S	TA	X	Y		
Strata	BWC-O	—	—	—	63	1	—	—	—	—	222	46	332	13.5
	BWC-S	34	193	—	—	—	27	—	2	—	—	—	256	10.4
	IMP-O	—	—	—	38	—	—	—	—	7	1	—	46	1.9
	IMP-S	—	1	—	—	—	10	—	—	—	—	—	11	.4
	MCB-U	79	—	2	188	2	67	—	93	—	—	—	431	17.6
	MCB-W	1	—	—	1	—	21	—	—	—	—	—	23	.9
	SCB	50	1	10	172	2	352	5	105	—	—	—	697	28.4
	TRIB	88	2	3	8	—	22	—	—	—	—	—	123	5.0
	TWZ	5	43	—	186	—	294	7	—	—	—	—	535	21.8
Total catch, by gear		257	240	15	656	5	793	12	200	7	223	46	2,454	NA
Percentage of total catch, by gear		10.5	9.8	0.6	26.7	0.2	32.3	0.5	8.1	0.3	9.1	1.9	NA	100.0

Trends in Distribution and Abundance

Total numbers of bighead carp caught by the Long Term Resource Monitoring Program have increased from one individual in Pool 26 of the Mississippi River in 1991 to a high of 1,297 individuals from the Open River Reach and Pool 26 of the Mississippi River and La Grange Reach of the Illinois River, combined, in 2000 (fig. 26). Bighead carp numbers were highest in 2000 due to high reproductive success in 2000, and many young-of-year individuals were collected in all three Program reaches where they occur (fig. 27) (Chick and Pegg, 2001). A large percentage of these bighead carp matured in 2003 (Long Term Resource Monitoring Program, written commun., 2002).

Ecologic and Economic Impacts

Because they are large planktivorious filter feeders, bighead carp may impact other native filter feeders such as paddlefish, gizzard shad, and buffalo fish (*Ictiobus* spp.) as well as larval and juvenile fish of all other species when they occupy similar habitats (Benson and others, 2001; Chick and

Pegg, 2001). When introduced, bighead carp have shown to negatively affect native filter-feeding fishes in Thailand (de Iongh and Van Zon, 1993). In addition, Schrank and others, (2003) have shown that age-0 bighead carp have a competitive advantage over native age-0 paddlefish within experimental mesocosms.

The fishing industry economy can be affected directly if bighead carp suppress paddlefish and buffalo fisheries in the Upper Mississippi River System and a market for bighead carp does not develop. The commercial value of paddlefish and buffalo in the Illinois River in 2001 was $131,500 (Maher, 2002). As of 2001, bighead and silver carp accounted for 2.4 percent of the estimated value of the commercial fishery in Illinois (all waters) with a total of 140,385 kg or 5 percent of the total commercial harvest by weight in Illinois (Maher, 2002). As with silver carp, bighead carp have been introduced throughout the world, and there is evidence that these introductions have led to decreased species diversity and abundance in commercial catches (Spataru and Gophen, 1985; Sugunan, 1997; Petr, 2002). When bighead carp compete for food with young fish, species important to the local recreational fishing economy may be suppressed.

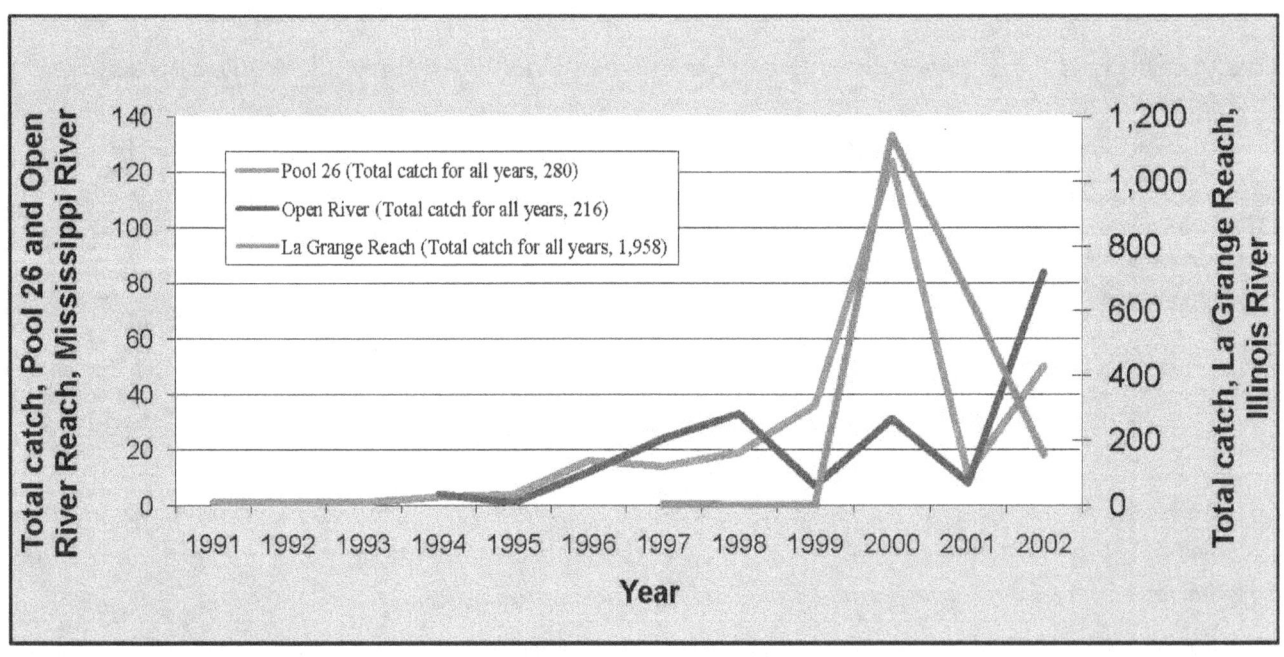

Figure 26.   Long Term Resource Monitoring Program total annual catch of bighead carp *Hypophthalmichthys nobilis* by study reach from 1989 to 2002.

Discussion

The native distribution of bighead carp in China and established populations elsewhere in Asia suggest that this species may be able to establish populations as far north as Pool 1 of the Mississippi River in the vicinity of Minneapolis and St. Paul, Minn., based solely upon latitude and water temperatures. Bighead carp have been introduced to at least 71 countries (Kolar and others, 2007). The likelihood of competition of this species with other filter feeders, as well as the plankton-dependent young of year of many native species, is high. High local abundances in side channels and tributaries, as observed in La Grange Reach of the Illinois River and the Open River Reach of the Mississippi River, suggest that bighead carp will probably affect the food web, at least within these areas of concentration. Bighead carp have potential as a food fish, marketed whole or canned, and could be potentially competitive with the tuna market (Stone and others, 2000). Bighead carp and silver carp are "the most intensively cultured fish species in Asia" (Xie and Yang, 2000). Bighead carp is fourth in global annual production (Stone and others, 2000). Given the high abundance of more traditional sport fish in the Upper Mississippi River System and a cultural preference for these species, angling for bighead carp may not have the same value as it does in European rivers and in China, where it is caught with baits made of dough and paste (Welcomme, 1981; Jennings, 1988). Young-of-year and juvenile silver carp and, to some degree, bighead carp look similar to gizzard shad and threadfin shad and are often collected together to be used as bait. It is likely these Asian carp could be introduced in other waters if anglers use them as bait. For this reason, South Dakota changed its laws to make it illegal to collect bait from below Gavins Point Dam (South Dakota 2004 Fishing Regulations, 2004).

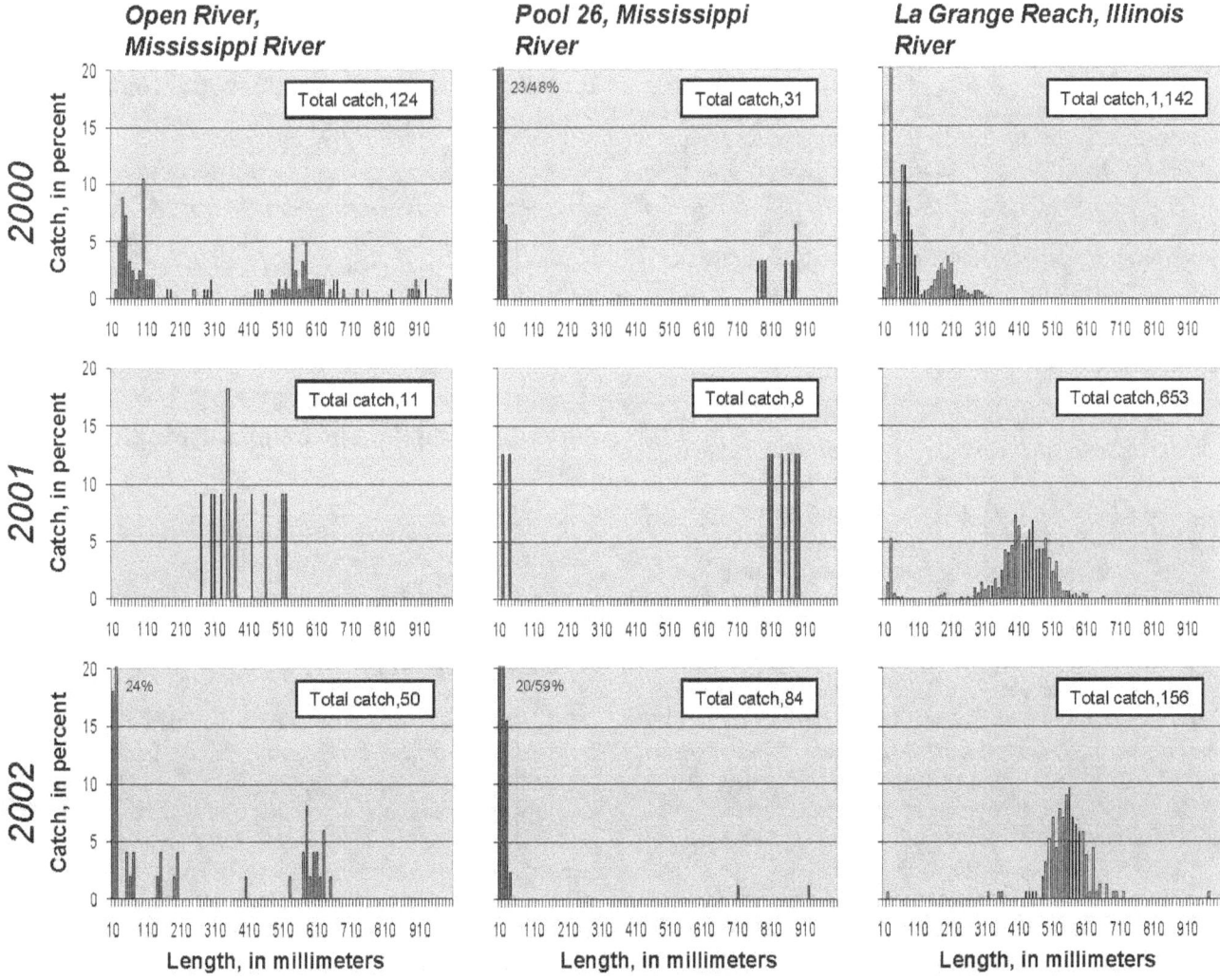

Figure 27.   Percentage of total bighead carp *Hypophthalmichthys nobilis* catch by 10-millimeter increments (length distribution) within three Long Term Resource Monitoring Program study reaches from 2000 to 2002.

Rudd *Scardinius erythrophthalmus*

Native Range Biology

The native range of the rudd includes Western Europe, Asia Minor, the Aral Sea Basin, and the southern coast of the Caspian Sea (Berg, 1964; Robins and others, 1991). The rudd is most often found in slow-moving vegetated rivers and lakes, but has also been found in brackish water (Laird and Page, 1996).

Rudd prefer warmwater lakes or medium to large rivers with slow-moving pools.

Photograph by Robert M. McDowall

Adult maturity occurs at age-3, with a life span of approximately 11 years. Spawning occurs from May through July at water temperatures of 18 to 27°C. Females produce 96,000 to 232,000 eggs that can be attached to vegetation in shallow water (Froese and Pauly, 2004). Total length of rudd can range from 20 to 30 cm and weigh from 198 to 397 g (Berg, 1964). Rudd can be easily confused with golden shiner (Crossman and others, 1992; Hirsch, 1998).

Pathway of Introduction

The earliest verified introduction date for the rudd in the United States is 1916, but rudd may have been introduced into Central Park Lake in New York City as early as 1897 (Bean, 1897; Hubbs, 1921; Burkhead and Williams, 1991). Page and Burr (1991) report established rudd populations still survive in New York and Maine. However, because they were propagated as a bait species by the fish farming industry in Arkansas in the early 1980s, the rudd has been recorded as introduced to public waters in 20 states. The Ontario Ministry of Natural Resources has reported rudd in the Ontario waters of St. Lawrence River, as well as Lakes Ontario and Erie (Crossman and others, 1992; Dextrase, 2001). Flooding of rearing ponds in Arkansas in 1987 also contributed to wild populations (Pflieger, 1997). Further evidence suggests it is established in Massachusetts, Nebraska, South Dakota, and Washington (U.S. Geological Survey, 2004; Nico and Fuller, 2005). The rudd is known from several locations in Illinois, including the Kaskaskia, Fox, and Illinois Rivers, and from several sites within Missouri, including the Missouri River (Burr and others, 1996; Laird and Page, 1996; Rasmussen, 2002).

Distribution in Long Term Resource Monitoring Program Study Reaches

Two rudd were collected by Long Term Resource Monitoring Program staff in Pool 13 in 1999 (fig. 29), although there is some question about the positive identification of the two specimens due to the small and deteriorated state of the fish when identified (Robert Hrabik, Missouri Department of Conservation, oral commun., 2002). No other rudd have been collected by the Program.

Relation of Habitat and Sampling Method to Fish Catch

The only occurrence of rudd in Long Term Resource Monitoring Program collections was in a shoreline seine performed in the impounded section of Pool 13 in 1999.

Ecological Impacts

Burkhead and Williams (1991) demonstrated in a laboratory setting that rudd could easily hybridize with native golden shiners. Based on these results, they hypothesized that rudd may produce offspring with wild populations of the golden shiner. Rudd could also affect inland waters by increasing nutrient loading due to ineffectively processing plant material, depleting aquatic vegetation areas necessary for spawning and nursery areas for other species, and disrupting native predator-prey relationships (Hirsch, 1998). Cadwallader (1977)

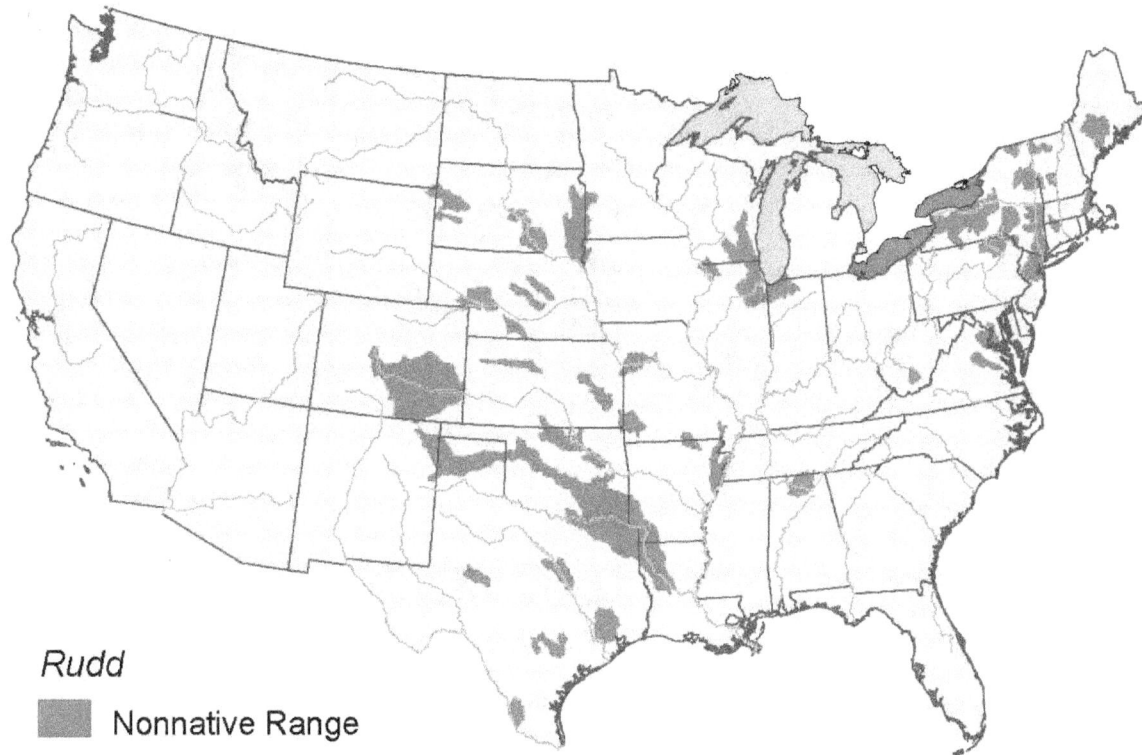

Figure 28. Distribution of rudd *Scardinius erythrophthalmus* in the United States.

reviewed the potential impacts of rudd in waters of North Island, New Zealand. He concluded, in part, that rudd could be expected to compete for invertebrate food sources with native fishes. If the rudd becomes established in the Upper Mississippi River System, it may compete with native fish populations, potentially altering ecosystems (Laird and Page, 1996).

Discussion

In 1986, rudd was listed among species with declining populations in the United States, probably because fisheries managers were unaware of the recent and rapid spread of the species by fish farmers (Courtenay and others, 1986; Burkhead and Williams, 1991). Rudd may also thrive in areas that are polluted or eutrophic (Cadwallader, 1977; Nico and Fuller, 2005).

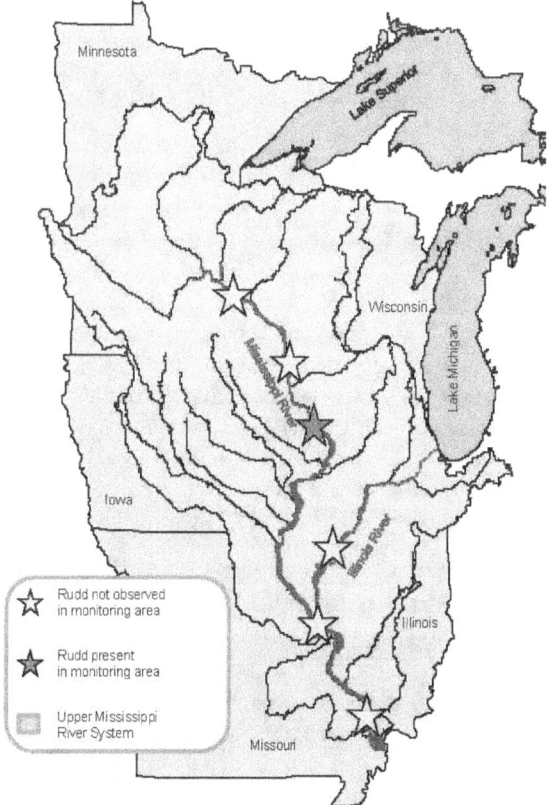

Figure 29. Long Term Resource Monitoring Program study reaches where rudd *Scardinius erythrophthalmus* were collected within the Upper Mississippi River System Basin from 1989 to 2002.

Muskellunge *Esox masquinongy*

Native Range Biology

The native range of the muskellunge stretches throughout the eastern portion of North America. Muskellunge are reported as being native to Indiana, Iowa, Kentucky, Maine, Michigan, Minnesota, New Hampshire, New York, North Carolina, North Dakota, Ohio, Pennsylvania, South Dakota, Tennessee, Vermont, West Virginia, Wisconsin, and the Provinces of Manitoba, Ontario, and Quebec, Canada (Lee and others, 1980). Although muskellunge have a wide native range, their populations are often supplemented by intentional stocking in many areas (for example, Alabama, Arkansas, Delaware, District of Columbia, Georgia, Illinois, Maryland, Missouri, Nebraska, New Jersey, Virginia, and New Brunswick, Canada). In Wisconsin waters, muskellunge will grow on average to 760 mm in length in 5 years and in 15 years can reach lengths over 1,200 mm (Oehmcke and others, 1965; Becker, 1983). Muskellunge spawn during spring in water temperatures of 9 to 15°C (Etnier and Starnes, 1993). They spawn indiscriminately, strewing their eggs over the bottom of the water body, and a single female may lay up to 180,000 eggs (Oehmcke and others, 1965). Peak feeding temperature is 17.2°C, and feeding declines in water temperatures above 29.4°C; the preferred prey of muskellunge includes yellow perch, suckers, and small minnows (Becker, 1983).

Pathway of Introduction

Muskellunge is native to some Ohio River drainage basins, including Cumberland and Tennessee Rivers, Upper Mississippi River System drainage basins, the Great Lakes, southern Hudson Bay tributaries, and some northern Atlantic Coastal drainage basins (fig. 30) (Etnier and Starnes, 1993). However, Becker (1983) notes the absence of muskellunge below Lake Pepin (Pool 4 of the Mississippi River) in recent years. They are intentionally stocked for sport fishing.

Distribution in Long Term Resource Monitoring Program Study Reaches

Only one catch of a muskellunge has been reported by Long Term Resource Monitoring Program field crews. In late summer 1996, the Open River Reach Field Station crew caught one muskellunge in the Big Muddy River, a tributary to the Mississippi River (fig. 31).

Photograph by Mike McClelland, Illinois Natural History Survey, Illinois River Biological Station

Relation of Habitat and Sampling Method to Fish Catch

The single muskellunge specimen was caught in a Mississippi River tributary in a large hoop net.

Economic and Ecological Impacts

Muskellunge are regarded as one of the more exciting game fish in North America (Trautman, 1981). The economic value of muskellunge fishing to resort, sporting goods, and associated business is high (Becker, 1983). Many anglers participate in muskellunge fishing, but pollution, habitat alteration, and introduction of nonnative species are believed to be the primary threats to the existence of muskellunge in its native range (Trautman, 1981). However, muskellunge are large predators and may reduce the numbers of other game species when they are introduced to a closed system (Gammon and Hasler, 1965; Tomelleri and Eberle, 1990).

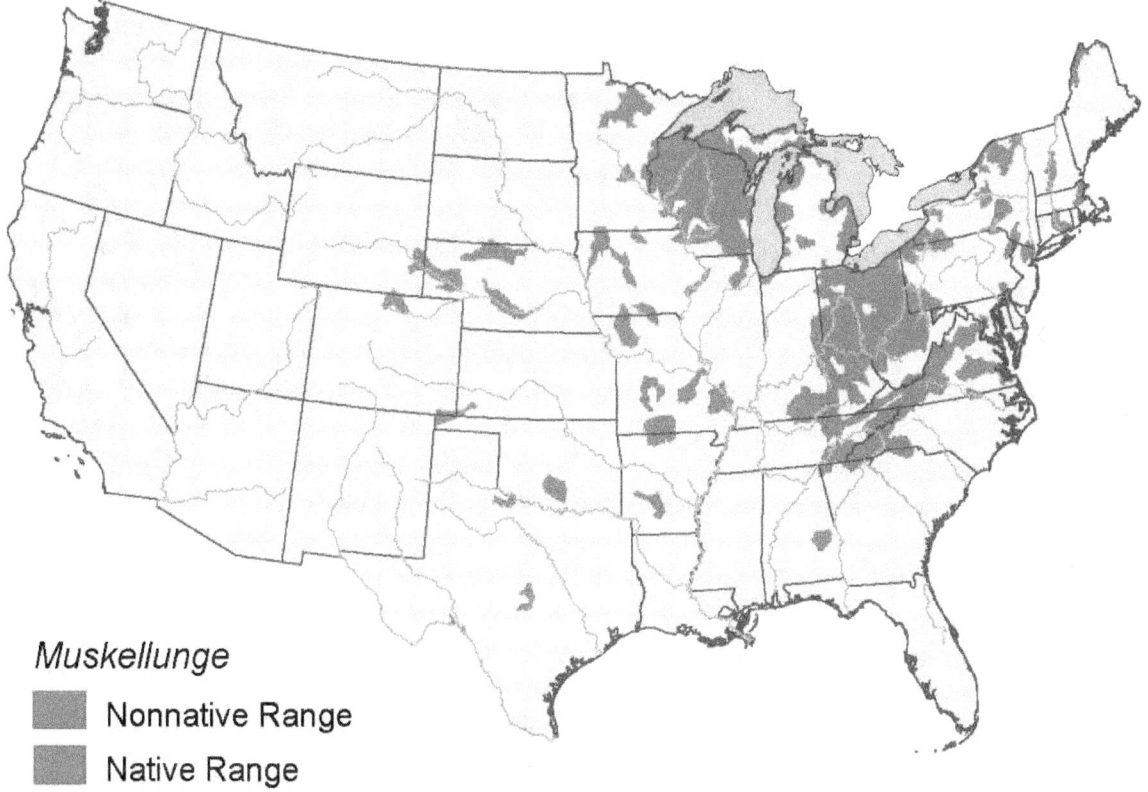

Muskellunge

Nonnative Range

Native Range

Figure 30. Distribution of muskellunge *Esox masquinongy* in the United States.

Discussion

The muskellunge is native to the upper portions of the Upper Mississippi River System, but they have been intentionally stocked for sport fishing in many other locations, and this introduction is probably responsible for occurrences detected by the Long Term Resource Monitoring Program in the lower study reaches. Although the muskellunge is not a nonnative species in the strictest sense, because of the stocking efforts throughout the Upper Mississippi River System states, the resulting impacts are similar to other nonnative species outside the native range.

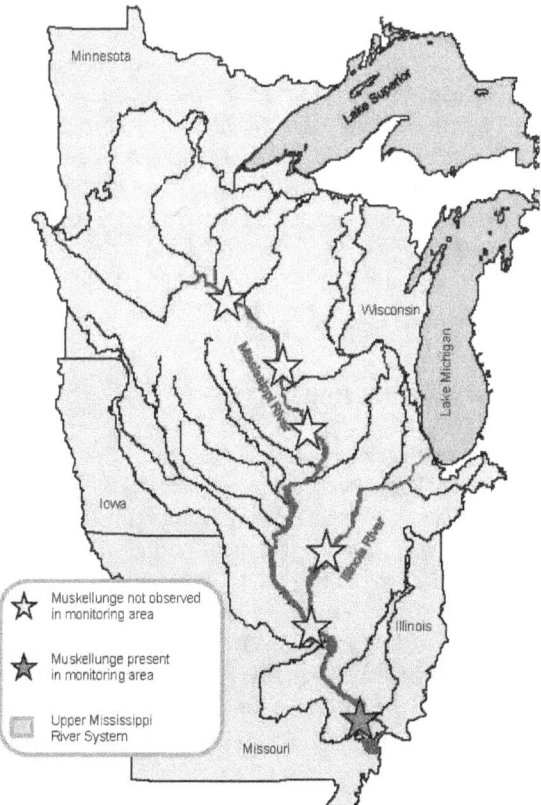

Figure 31. Long Term Resource Monitoring Program study reaches where muskellunge *Esox masquinongy* were collected within the Upper Mississippi River System Basin from 1989 to 2002.

Tiger Muskellunge *Esox masquinongy* x *E. lucius*

Photograph by Kevin Irons, Illinois Natural History Survey, Illinois River Biological Station

Native Range Biology

The tiger muskellunge is a hybrid between northern pike and muskellunge (Tomelleri and Eberle, 1990). The native range of the tiger muskellunge occurs where northern pike and muskellunge occupy the same waters. Muskellunge and northern pike are reported as being native to Iowa, Maine, Michigan, Minnesota, New Hampshire, New York, North Dakota, Ohio, Pennsylvania, South Dakota, Vermont, Wisconsin, and the Provinces of Manitoba, Ontario and Quebec, Canada (Lee and others, 1980). Natural hybridization occurs rarely throughout the range; however, Oehmcke and others, (1965) documented natural hybrid muskellunge making up 40–50 percent of "muskellunge" in a few lake systems. Most tiger muskellunge populations result from the intentional crossbreeding of a male northern pike with a female muskellunge by hatcheries throughout the United States (Black and Williamson, 1946). These hybrids have been reportedly stocked in more than 30 states (fig. 32). The results of these hybridizations create sterile males and females that can be fertile (Becker, 1983). Tiger muskellunge do not reach the maximum lengths of muskellunge (1,200 mm) but grow faster and are more robust (Scott and Crossman, 1973). Spawning requirements resemble those of the parental stocks. Tiger muskellunge spawn during the spring in water temperatures of 9 to 15°C (Etnier and Starnes, 1993). They spawn indiscriminately, strewing their eggs over the bottom of the water body, and a single female may extrude up to 180,000 eggs (Oehmcke and others, 1965). Peak feeding temperature is 17.2°C, and feeding declines in water temperatures above 29.4°C (Becker, 1983).

Pathway of Introduction

Tiger muskellunge most likely are present within the Upper Mississippi River System due to direct stocking efforts within the basin and not natural hybridization. Although northern pike are relatively common within the northern part of the river system, muskellunge are relatively rare (only one was collected by Long Term Resource Monitoring Program) and are probably the result of stocking efforts. Because more than 30 states stock tiger muskellunge, the potential for escapement from these intentionally stocked waters is high.

Distribution in Long Term Resource Monitoring Program Study Reaches

Occurrences of tiger muskellunge in Long Term Resource Monitoring Program collections were confined to La Grange Reach of the Illinois River (fig. 33). Four specimens have been reported: one each in 1992 and 1994 and two in 1997. All four specimens were caught in the late summer or early fall.

Relation of Habitat and Sampling Method to Fish Catch

The first tiger muskellunge collected by the Long Term Resource Monitoring Program was collected by use of daytime electrofishing in backwater, contiguous-shoreline habitat. The second tiger muskellunge was also collected from backwater, contiguous-shoreline, but it was collected in a fyke net. The third tiger muskellunge was collected in a minnow fyke net deployed in main channel border-unstructured habitat. The final tiger muskellunge was caught within the tailwater zone by night electrofishing.

Ecological Impacts

In general, tiger muskellunge prosper in clean, clear lakes with abundant underwater structure and vegetation used for cover and feeding (Etnier and Starnes, 1993). If stocking rates and escapement into the Upper Mississippi River System increase, tiger muskellunge may negatively affect northern pike and other game fish populations by direct competition for food, because they are thermally more tolerant than northern pike or muskellunge and exhibit high growth rates (Scott, 1964).

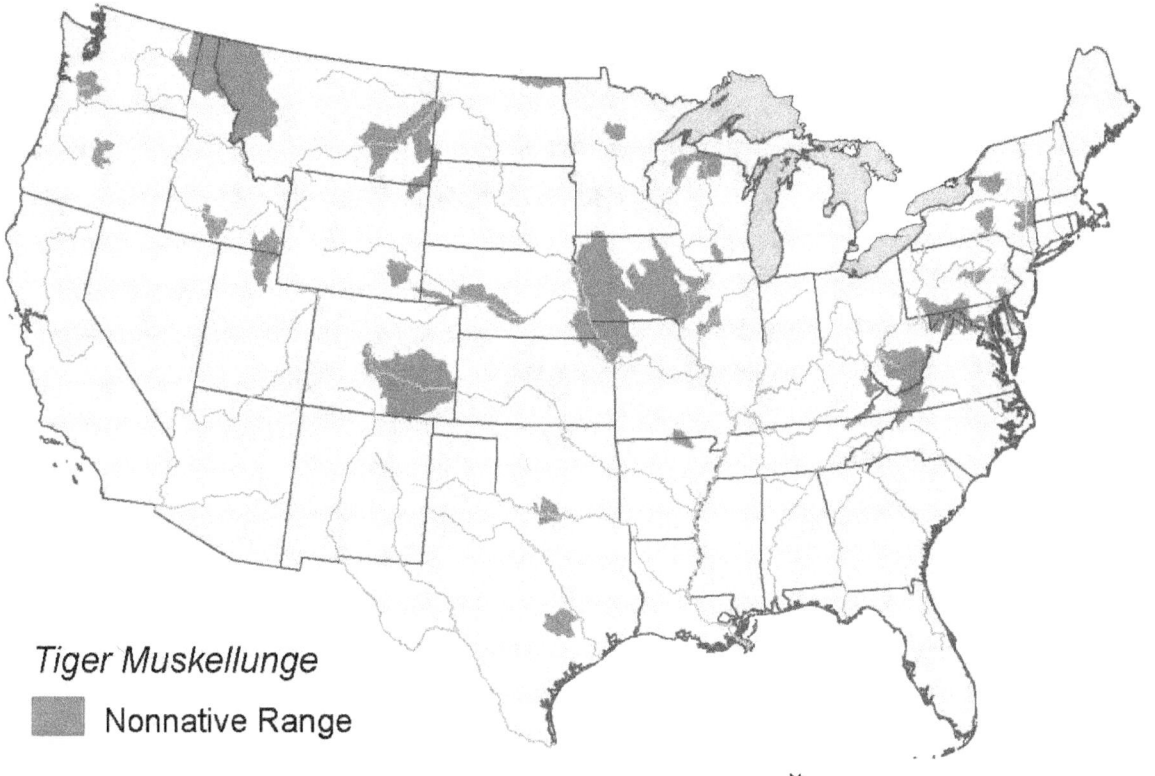

Figure 32. Distribution of nonnative tiger muskellunge *Esox masquinongy x E. lucius* in the United States.

Discussion

Many anglers regard tiger muskellunge as a prized game fish. Known for their stamina, tiger muskellunge are considered to be one of the more difficult catches. They are often stocked in areas where northern pike and muskellunge are absent (Becker, 1983). Tiger muskellunge grow fast, and in managed populations, without parental species, tiger muskellunge will not reproduce. This makes the tiger muskellunge ideal for managers, who then can control the abundance of this predator by stocking rates. Tiger muskellunge are often stocked in waters that have heavy fishing pressure, such as those near large cities.

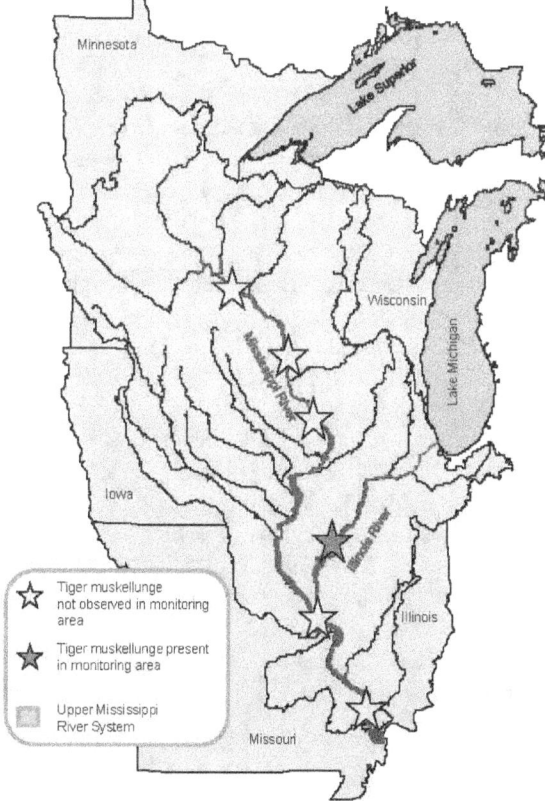

Figure 33. Long Term Resource Monitoring Program study reaches where tiger muskellunge *Esox masquinongy x E. lucius* were collected within the Upper Mississippi River System Basin from 1989 to 2002.

Rainbow Smelt *Osmerus mordax*

Native Range Biology

The native range of the rainbow smelt is Atlantic drainages from Newfoundland to the Delaware River, Pennsylvania, and Arctic and Pacific drainages to Vancouver Island, British Columbia, Canada (Page and Burr, 1991) (fig. 34). The rainbow smelt is an anadromous species that leaves coastal waters to ascend streams to spawn from late March through early May. Indigenous, landlocked populations do occur in lakes in northeastern North America (Scott and Crossman. 1973). The maximum size of adult rainbow smelt varies from 100 mm to over 350 mm in length among different water bodies (Scott and Crossman, 1973). Rainbow smelt generally spawn when water temperature rises above 4.4°C (Becker, 1983).

Photograph by Steve Delain, Minnesota Department of Natural Resources

Photograph by Wayne Nelson-Stastny, South Dakota Game Fish and Parks

Pathway of Introduction

The source of rainbow smelt in the Great Lakes, except possibly for Lake Ontario, appears to be Crystal Lake, Mich., which drains into Lake Michigan. This lake was stocked in 1912 with 16.4 million rainbow smelt from Green Lake, Maine (Van Oosten, 1937; Becker, 1983). Rainbow smelt in Lake Ontario, however, may have entered from Lake Erie by the Niagara River or the Welland Canal or may have been separately introduced (Christie, 1973). Smelt may have spread into the Mississippi River from Lake Michigan through the Chicago Sanitary and Ship Canal and Des Plaines River into the Illinois River (Burr and Mayden, 1980). Rainbow smelt have been collected in the Illinois River during fish sampling by the Illinois Natural History Survey before and after 1979. Alternatively, smelt may have gained access to the Mississippi River from a stocking in Lake Sakakawea, N. Dak., in 1971 as forage for salmonids (Mayden and others, 1987). Rainbow smelt spread down the Missouri River, reaching Missouri in 1978, and, in Pflieger's (1997) opinion, ultimately into the Mississippi River. Therefore, a combination of both canals and escapement from stocking events in North Dakota have likely assisted rainbow smelt in invasion of the Upper Mississippi River System.

Distribution in Long Term Resource Monitoring Program Study Reaches

Only one rainbow smelt has been collected by the Long Term Resource Monitoring Program. This 48-mm fish was recorded in 1993 from Pool 8 (fig. 35).

Relation of Habitat and Sampling Method to Fish Catch

The rainbow smelt was collected in a minnow fyke net deployed in main channel border- unstructured habitat.

Ecological Impacts

Hrabik and others, (1998) found that predation effects by rainbow smelt introduced into a lake included reductions in recruitment, declines in population, and the possible extirpation of some native species. Hrabik and others (1998) also found that competition for prey from introduced rainbow smelt could decrease the fitness of native species and ultimately reduce their population levels. In the Great Lakes, there is evidence that rainbow smelt compete with lake herring and other native whitefishes *Coregonus* spp. for food and that this competition may have played a role in their decline (Christie, 1973; Becker, 1983; Emery, 1985; Laird and Page, 1996). Evans and Loftus (1987) found that in 18 out of 26 case studies in which rainbow smelt were introduced into lakes they had negative effects on non-coevolved species. Although a few winter samples outside of the Long Term Resource Monitoring Program have been collected on reaches of the lower Mississippi River that have large numbers of young rainbow smelt, no adults have been found in either the Mississippi (Pflieger, 1997) or Missouri (Burr and Mayden, 1980) Rivers within the state of Missouri. These large numbers of young smelt are attributed to reproduction in upstream reservoirs of the Missouri River (Pflieger, 1997).

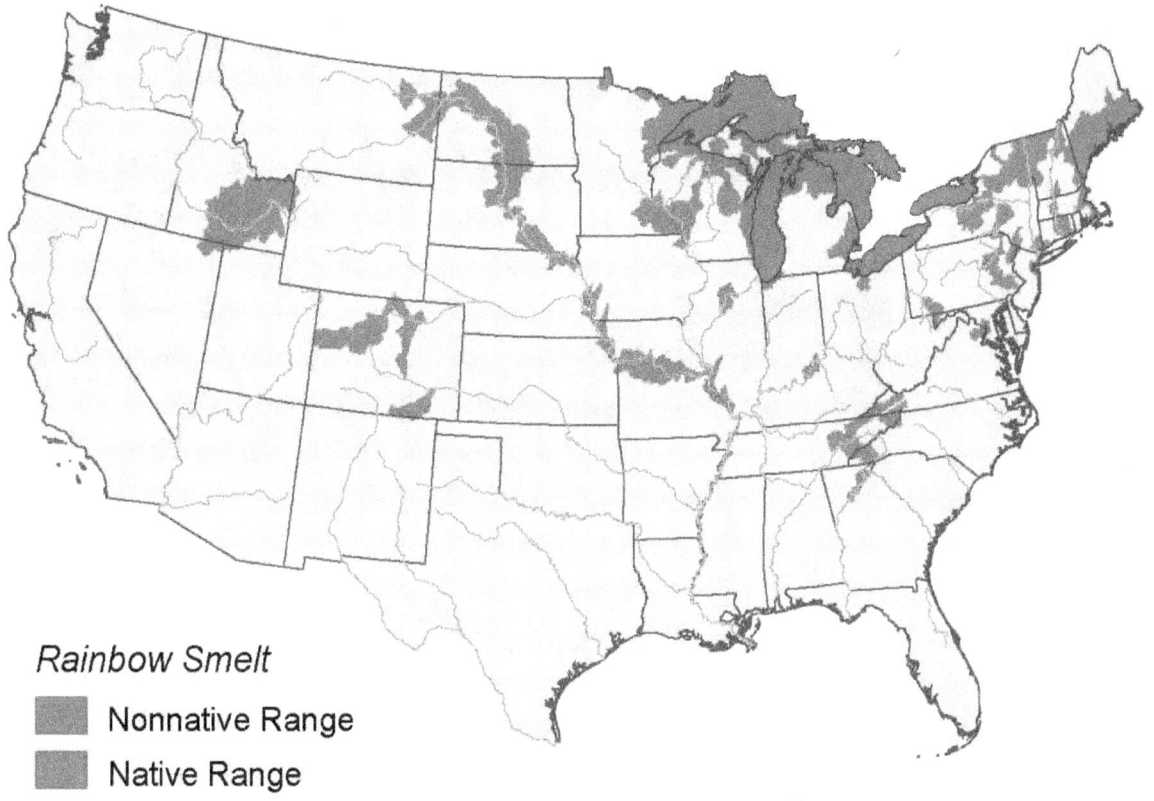

Rainbow Smelt

  Nonnative Range

  Native Range

Figure 34. Distribution of rainbow smelt *Osmerus mordax* in the United States.

Discussion

Rainbow smelt are established in the Great Lakes and have done so well that a commercial and sport fishery still exists to date. They have been collected in the Upper Mississippi River System in Illinois and Missouri, and are more common in winter samples than in samples collected during other seasons. It is unlikely that rainbow smelt could survive the late summer water temperatures in the Mississippi River, due to their preference for colder water (Hart and Ferguson, 1966; Laird and Page, 1996). As such, Pflieger (1997) concluded that populations in Missouri are maintained by immigration from upstream reservoirs on the Missouri River. In Missouri, rainbow smelt are less common today than they were 20 years ago and are more abundant in the Missouri River than the Mississippi River (Robert Hrabik, Missouri Department of Conservation, oral commun., 2002).

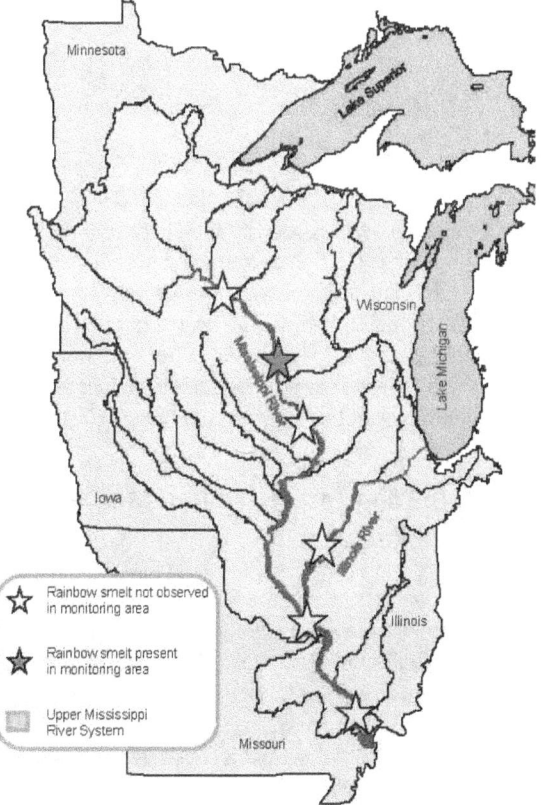

Figure 35. Long Term Resource Monitoring Program study reaches where rainbow smelt *Osmerus mordax* were collected within the Upper Mississippi River System Basin from 1989 to 2002.

Brown Trout *Salmo trutta*

Photograph by the Minnesota Department of Natural Resources

Native Range Biology

The native range of brown trout is all of Europe, the Atlas Mountains of North Africa, and eastward to the Ural Mountains of Russia and the tributaries of the Black and Caspian Seas in western Asia (Stolz and Schnell, 1991). Record brown trout in large rivers, lake, or sea environments can achieve sizes up to 1,000 mm in length and 18 kg in weight, however in small streams they commonly reach only 450 mm in length and 1.0 kg in weight (Scott and Crossman, 1973). The brown trout spawns in fall or early winter, creating redds or nests within gravel of riffles. Redds generally contain 400–3,000 eggs that hatch in roughly 50 days. The brown trout tolerates higher stream temperature than native brook trout and in general is less vulnerable to angling than the rainbow trout (Becker, 1983; Pflieger, 1997).

Pathway of Introduction

The brown trout was first imported into the United States in 1883 from Central Europe (Becker, 1983). In 1884, 4,900 brown trout fry were stocked into the Pere Marquette River, Mich., and this is the first documented introduction of brown trout into United States waters. After this initial stocking, the intentional distribution of brown trout by other agencies throughout much of the United States continued. At least 34 states (fig. 36) and several Canadian provinces have naturalized populations of brown trout (Bachman. 1991).

Distribution in Long Term Resource Monitoring Program Study Reaches

Of the six Long Term Resource Monitoring Program study reaches, brown trout were present in three, Pools 4, 8, and 13 of the Mississippi River (fig. 37). Brown trout are widely distributed in coldwater tributaries to the Upper Mississippi River System. One brown trout was collected in 1992 in Pool 4; five were collected in Pool 8 (one each in 1993, 1994, 1996, 1997, and 1998); and one was collected in 1995 in Pool 13.

Relation of Habitat and Sampling Method to Fish Catch

Brown trout have been collected in main channel border-unstructured, tailwater zone, impounded habitat-shoreline, and backwater, contiguous-offshore habitats (table 8).

Ecological Impacts

The introduction of brown trout has been linked to the decline of native fish populations, especially other salmonids, through predation and competition for food and space (Taylor and others, 1984). Fausch and White (1986) found that native adult brook trout were displaced by adult brown trout from preferred habitats in a Michigan stream and in the northeastern United States as a whole. Other studies have demonstrated deleterious effects from the introduction of brown trout on Dolly Varden (Moyle, 1976), golden trout (Krueger and May, 1991), and cutthroat trout (Behnke, 1992). Becker (1983) suggests that brown trout do not occur in the Mississippi River, and at low abundances they would not affect native fish populations. The Long Term Resource Monitoring Program collections suggest that the Mississippi River may minimally provide a pathway for brown trout to travel when water temperatures are low and, thus, move from one stream to another. This potential pathway should be considered if a stream management alternative within the Upper Mississippi River System calls for exclusion of brown trout.

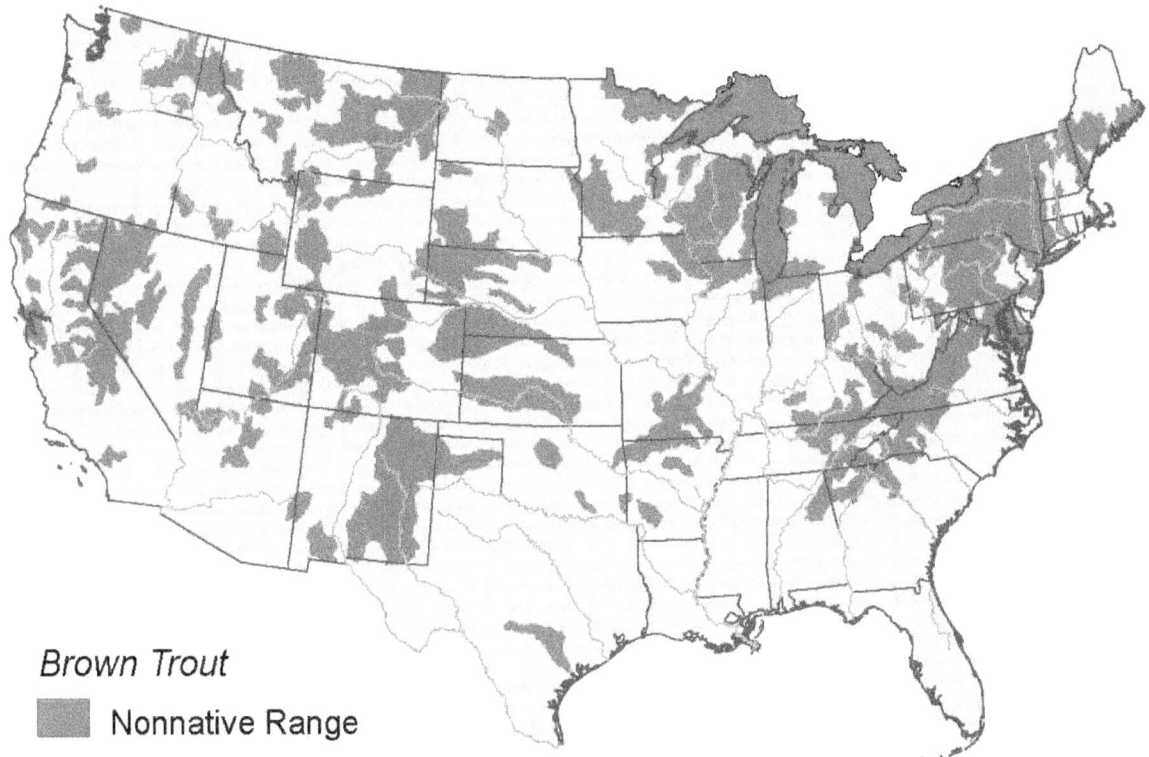

Brown Trout

■ Nonnative Range

Figure 36. Distribution of brown trout *Salmo trutta* in the United States.

Discussion

Periodic stocking of brown trout is necessary for maintaining populations in many states. In streams of Wisconsin, southeastern Minnesota, and northeastern Iowa, natural reproduction of brown trout has increased. A documented increase in naturally reproducing brown trout in these three states is mainly attributed to improvements in land-use practices and stream habitat (Thorn and others, 1997). The ability of brown trout to survive elevated water temperatures, loss of successive year classes, and most importantly, intense angling pressure has made it one of North America's most successful salmonids (Bachman, 1991). For these reasons, anglers and resource managers continue to create and manage fisheries for this nonnative by use of habitat projects and hatchery programs. Although they are present in many of the cold-water tributary streams of the Upper Mississippi River System, brown trout will probably continue to be found only intermittently in Long Term Resource Monitoring Program catches because of their preference for cooler water than that found in the Mississippi River year round. The Mississippi River may provide this species with a dispersal pathway for movement within the river system, however.

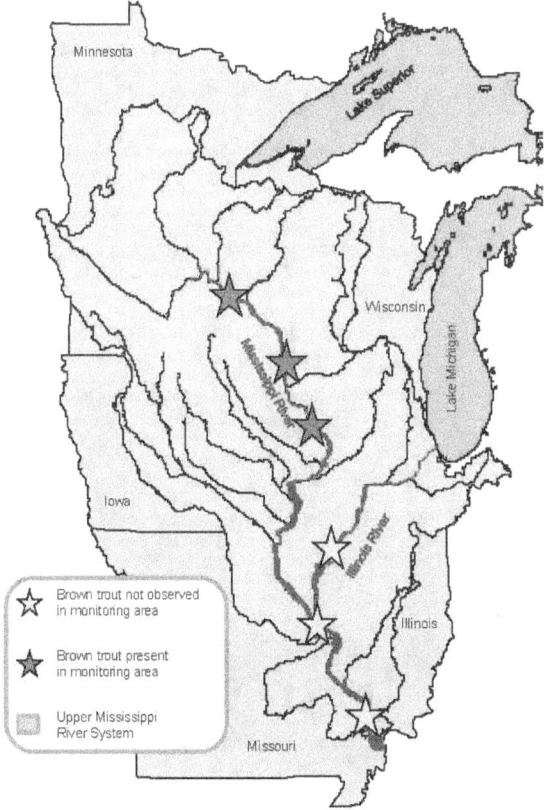

Figure 37. Long Term Resource Monitoring Program study reaches where brown trout *Salmo trutta* were collected within the Upper Mississippi River System Basin from 1989 to 2002.

Table 8.   Brown trout *Salmo trutta* total catch, by strata and gear, collected by the Long Term Resource Monitoring Program from 1989 to 2002.

[Strata abbreviations: BWC-O, backwater, contiguous-offshore; IMP-S, impounded habitat-shoreline; MCB-U, main channel border-unstructured; TWZ, tailwater zone-400 meters below dam. Gear abbreviations: F, fyke net; M, minnow fyke net; NEF, night electrofishing; X, tandem fyke net-offshore. —, no catch; NA, not applicable]

		Gear				Total catch, by strata	Percentage of total catch, by strata
		F	M	NEF	X		
Strata	BWC-O	—	—	—	1	1	14.3
	IMP-S	1	1	—	—	2	28.6
	MCB-U	—	—	1	—	1	14.3
	TWZ	—	—	3	—	3	42.9
	Total catch, by gear	1	1	4	1	7	NA
	Percentage of total catch, by gear	14.3	14.3	57.1	14.3	NA	100.0

White Perch *Morone americana*

Photograph by Kevin Irons, Illinois Natural History Survey, Illinois River Biological Station

Native Range Biology

The native range of the white perch is confined to the East Coast of North America, from the upper St. Lawrence River south to South Carolina (Scott and Crossman, 1973; Laird and Page, 1996; Pflieger, 1997) (fig. 38). It is known to be semianadromous, moving inland from the Atlantic Ocean primarily during spawning. White perch can tolerate changing environmental and salinity conditions such as those in the lower Hudson River. However, they can remain in freshwater year round as well (Hergenrader and Bliss, 1971; Bath and O'Connor, 1982).

White perch spawn in spring when water temperatures range from 11 to 15°C (Sheri and Power, 1968) over various substrates (Scott and Crossman, 1973). Females carry from 15,000 to 300,000 eggs (Sheri and Power, 1968; Scott and Crossman, 1973; Bath and O'Connor, 1982). The eggs are adhesive and hatch in less than 6 days (Scott and Crossman, 1973; Boileau, 1985). White perch eat mainly insects and crustaceans, shifting primarily to fish and fish eggs seasonally (Schaeffer and Margraf, 1987; Parrish and Margraf, 1994; Irons and others, 2002). Reid (1972) also showed that diet shifted from insects and crustaceans to fish based upon overall body length. Large adult white perch range from 330 to 450 mm (Scott and Crossman, 1973).

Pathway of Introduction

White perch began to establish inland populations through the series of canals within the state of New York in about 1900. White perch became established in the Great Lakes, in Lakes Erie and Ontario, in about 1950 (Scott and Christie, 1963). White perch continued to expand its range in the Midwest and throughout the Great Lakes (fig. 38) (Larsen, 1954; Christie, 1973; Ver Duin, 1984; Johnson and Evans, 1990; Cochran and Hesse, 1994). White perch were collected in the proximity of Chicago, Ill., in Lake Michigan in 1988 (Savitz and others, 1989). The Illinois Natural History Survey collected white perch in the Upper Mississippi River System, Middle Illinois River in 1991 (Irons and others, 2002). White perch were first collected the following year by Long Term Resource Monitoring Program in La Grange Reach of the Illinois River. Subsequent collections have documented the spread of white perch throughout La Grange Reach of the Illinois River and their expansion into Pool 26 in 1999 (Irons and others, 2002; Long Term Resource Monitoring Program written commun., 2002). Although they have not been documented in Program collections from the Open River Reach to date, white perch have been documented by other researchers to be present there (Laird and Page, 1996; Pflieger, 1997). White perch have been stocked intentionally in Nebraska and unintentionally mixed with other *Morone* stocks in western states (Hergenrader and Bliss, 1971; Hergenrader, 1980).

Distribution in Long Term Resource Monitoring Program Study Reaches

White perch collections within the Upper Mississippi River System have been limited to the southern Long Term Resource Monitoring Program field stations (fig. 39), and 236 of 237 individuals were collected from 1989 to 2001 from La Grange Reach of the Illinois River. Field crews from the Program have collected only one white perch from Pool 26.

Relation of Habitat and Sampling Method to Fish Catch

White perch were first collected by the Long Term Resource Monitoring Program below Peoria Lock and Dam in 1992. This tailwater zone habitat alone accounts for 69.2 percent of 237 white perch collected by the Program. White perch have also been collected in backwater lakes (shoreline and offshore combined; 23.6 percent), main channel border-unstructured (4.2 percent), side channel border (2.5 percent), and impounded habitat-offshore (0.4 percent).

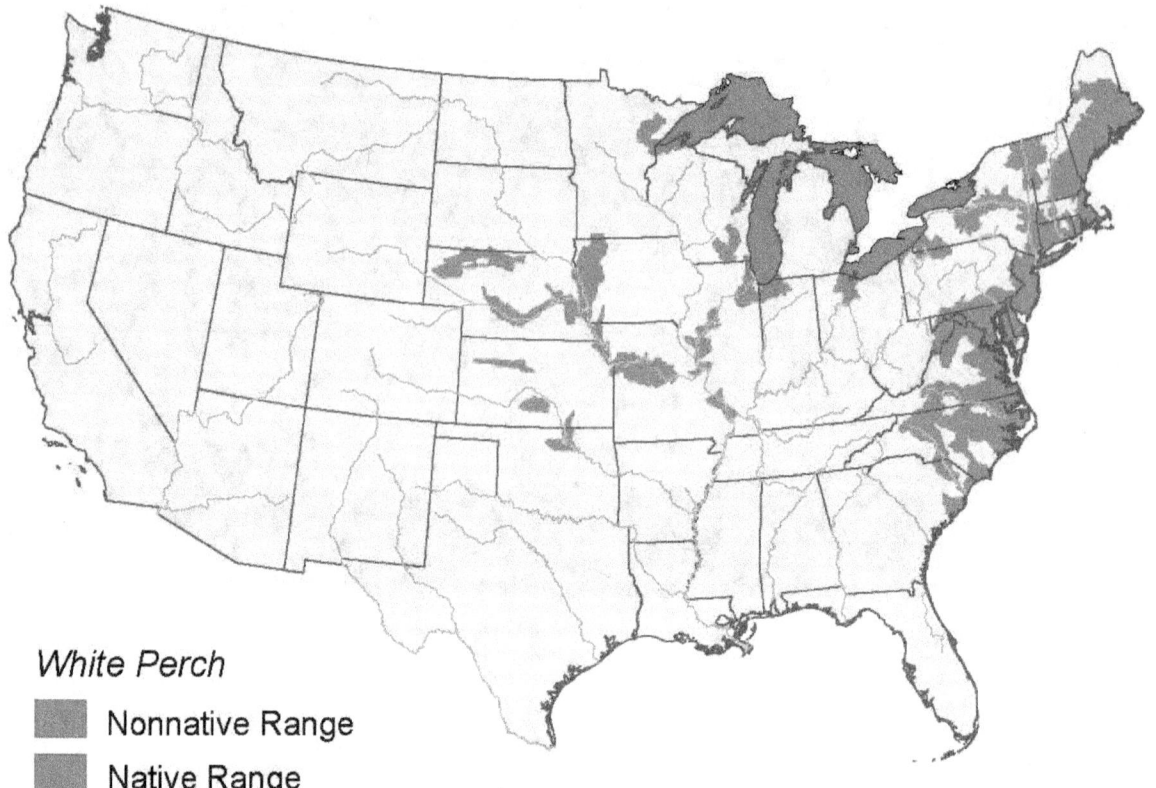

White Perch

Nonnative Range

Native Range

Figure 38. Distribution of white perch *Morone americana* in the United States.

Day and night electrofishing and fyke net account for 83.1 percent of white perch collected. The single individual from Pool 26 was collected in a tandem fyke net in the impounded area above the Mel Price Lock and Dam (table 9).

Trends in Distribution and Abundance

The number of white perch collected by Long Term Resource Monitoring Program sampling increased from two individuals in 1992 to a high of 54 individuals in 1999 (fig. 40). Abundance has remained fairly consistent since 1999, and the decrease in 2002 may have been due to gear allocation changes. Program sampling has also documented the expansion of this species, both to the south to Pool 26 in 1999 and into various habitats longitudinally within the Illinois River (Irons and others, 2002).

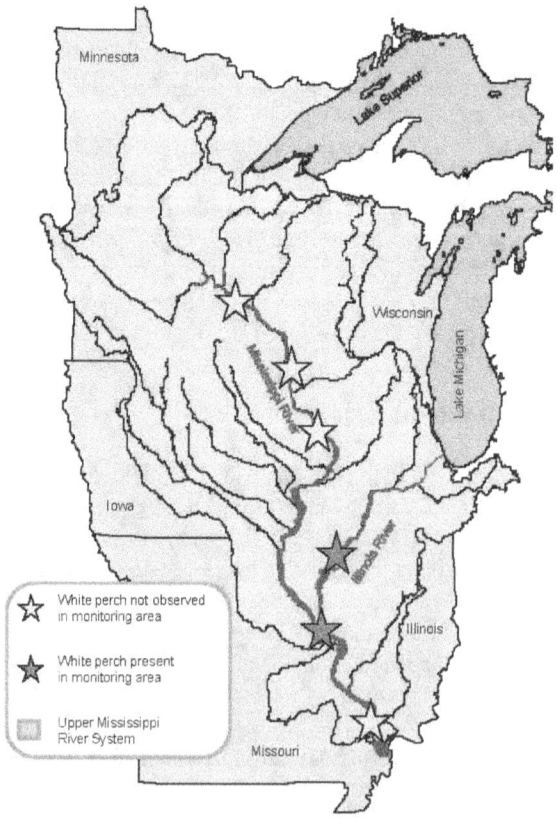

Figure 39. Long Term Resource Monitoring Program study reaches where white perch *Morone americana* were collected within the Upper Mississippi River System Basin from 1989 to 2002.

Table 9. White perch *Morone americana* total catch from 1989 to 2002, by strata and gear, collected by the Long Term Resource Monitoring Program.

[Strata abbreviations: BWC-O, backwater, contiguous-offshore; BWC-S, backwater, contiguous-shoreline; IMP-O, impounded habitat-offshore; MCB-U, main channel border-unstructured; SCB, side channel border; TWZ, tailwater zone-400 meters below dam. Gear abbreviations: DEF, day electrofishing; F, fyke net; HS, hoop net-small; M, minnow fyke net; NEF, night electrofishing; T, trawl; X, tandem fyke net-offshore; Y, tandem minnow fyke net-offshore. —, no catch; NA, not applicable]

		Gear								Total catch, by strata	Percentage of total catch, by strata
		DEF	F	HS	M	NEF	T	X	Y		
Strata	BWC-O	—	—	—	—	—	—	19	1	20	8.4
	BWC-S	6	27	—	3	—	—	—	—	36	15.2
	IMP-O	—	—	—	—	—	—	1	—	1	.4
	MCB-U	6	—	—	3	1	—	—	—	10	4.2
	SCB	5	—	—	1	—	—	—	—	6	2.5
	TWZ	24	66	1	9	62	2	—	—	164	69.2
Total catch, by gear		41	93	1	16	63	2	20	1	237	NA
Percentage of total catch, by gear		17.3	39.2	0.4	6.8	26.6	0.8	8.4	0.4	NA	100.0

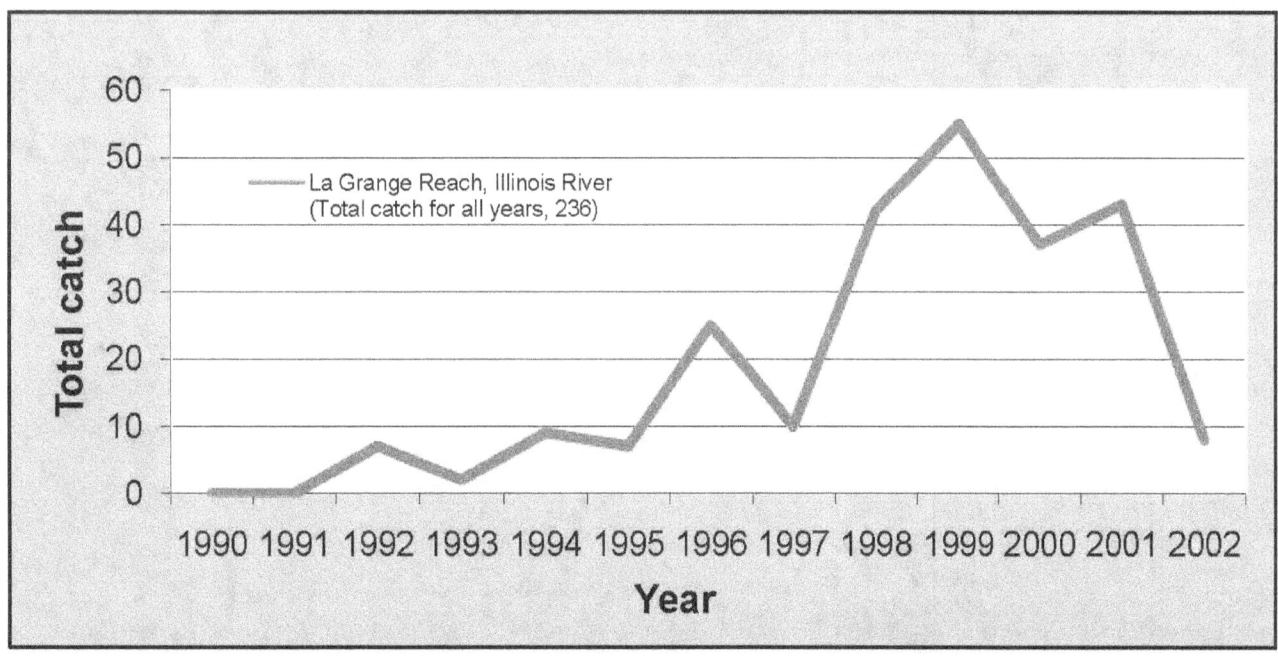

Figure 40. Long Term Resource Monitoring Program total annual catch of white perch *Morone americana* from La Grange Reach of the Illinois River from 1989 to 2002.

Ecological and Economic Impacts

White perch may have played an important role in reducing the recruitment of white bass in Lake Erie (Madenjian and others, 2000). White perch may therefore compete with native *Morone* spp. (white and yellow bass) in the Upper Mississippi River System, thus resulting in reduced recruitment. In addition, within the Upper Mississippi River System, the Long Term Resource Monitoring Program has identified white perch x yellow bass hybrids. Current research by the Illinois Natural History Survey is examining the extent of this phenomenon (Irons and others, 2002). White perch have been known to affect fish populations in Lake Erie by feeding on the eggs of other fish; in fact, fish eggs can, at times, make up nearly 100 percent of their diets while, during other times of year and life stage, white perch may feed on fish or insects (Schaeffer and Margraf, 1987; Parrish and Margraf, 1994). White perch can have direct effects on the food web. It has been noted that white perch can control amphipod abundance in eastern Lake Ontario (Hurley, 1992).

Further population growth of white perch in the Upper Mississippi River System could have economic effects if the abundances of native white and yellow bass decline because of their value as sport fish. White perch are commercially harvested both in its native range and in the Great Lakes (National Marine Fisheries Service, Fisheries Statistics Division, Silver Spring, Maryland, written commun., 2002; Scott and Crossman, 1973). It is unlikely that white perch will be of commercial value in the Upper Mississippi River System, however, because potential by-catch of other sport fish would not be acceptable. In addition, such a fishery probably would not greatly reduce white perch abundance because white perch are fecund (Boileau, 1985). The monetary value of a sport fishery for white perch in the Upper Mississippi River System would be expected to be lower than that of the native white bass, due to the smaller size of the white perch.

Discussion

The fact that white perch are found in northern clines in their native range suggests that they are climatically matched with the Upper Mississippi River System. Although dams may slow the spread of white perch (Cochran and Hesse, 1994), their preference for tailwater habitats will probably promote their movement north with water passed through dam locks, resulting in a slow spread throughout the river system. The Long Term Resource Monitoring Program has proven highly successful in documenting the spread of this nonnative fish. Attention by researchers and managers to habitat preference data may be able to reduce the impact of this invader in the Upper Mississippi River System (Jude and DeBoe, 1996; Irons and others, 2002).

Striped Bass *Morone saxatilis*

Native Range Biology

The native range of the striped bass is along the East Coast of North America from the St. Lawrence River in Canada to the St. Johns River in Florida; from the Suwannee River in western Florida to Lake Pontchartrain, Louisiana; and the open waters of the Atlantic Ocean (fig. 42) (Lee and others, 1980). Striped bass are primarily anadromous, inhabiting saltwater and migrating to freshwater to spawn (Ross, 2001). The impoundment of the Santee River in South Carolina during the 1940s resulted in a reproducing population adapted to a landlocked existence (Stevens, 1958). Offspring from these fish have been stocked in many inland waters of North America, where they generally inhabit reservoirs and the rivers that form them (Etnier and Starnes, 1993).

Spawning runs of striped bass in landlocked, freshwater populations begin when spring water temperatures approach 15°C (Etnier and Starnes, 1993). Striped bass have semibuoyant eggs that must be carried by currents of larger rivers for 36 to 75 hours before hatching (Pflieger, 1997). Young striped bass begin foraging on shrimp, crustaceans, worms, and insects, and adults consume mostly fish with occasional crabs and crustaceans (Scott and Crossman, 1973). Adults can reach 2 m in length and attain weights of up to 57 kg (Raney, 1952; Page and Burr, 1991).

Pathway of Introduction

Striped bass have been stocked throughout the United States (fig. 42), including the Pacific Coast of North America, where it was stocked in the late 1800s (Scott and Crossman, 1973). Striped bass have been introduced in scattered locations throughout the central United States. Many have been stocked in lakes and their associated tributary and outlet rivers. Some of these populations must be artificially maintained because of the lack of suitable spawning habitats. Spawning striped bass may travel great distances inland to spawn.

Striped bass were first collected in the Upper Mississippi River System by the Long Term Resource Monitoring Program in the Open River Reach in 1991. The first striped bass in La Grange Reach of the Illinois River observed by the Long Term Resource Monitoring Program was in 1994. Striped bass are occasionally found in the Illinois, Missouri, and Mississippi Rivers. In Missouri, striped bass have probably spawned in the Missouri River, yet most are likely escapees

Figure 41. A 14.5-kilogram striped bass collected from the Illinois River by the Long Term Resource Monitoring Program. (Kevin Irons, Illinois Natural History Survey, Illinois River Biological Station)

from stocked impoundments (Pflieger, 1997). It is possible that some individuals could have made the 980-mile trip to the lower Upper Mississippi River from the Gulf of Mexico.

Distribution in Long Term Resource Monitoring Program Study Reaches

Of the six Long Term Resource Monitoring Program study reaches, striped bass are present in the Open River Reach of the Mississippi River and La Grange Reach of the Illinois River (fig. 43). Forty of 59 individuals were collected in the Open River Reach. The remaining 19 individuals were collected in La Grange Reach.

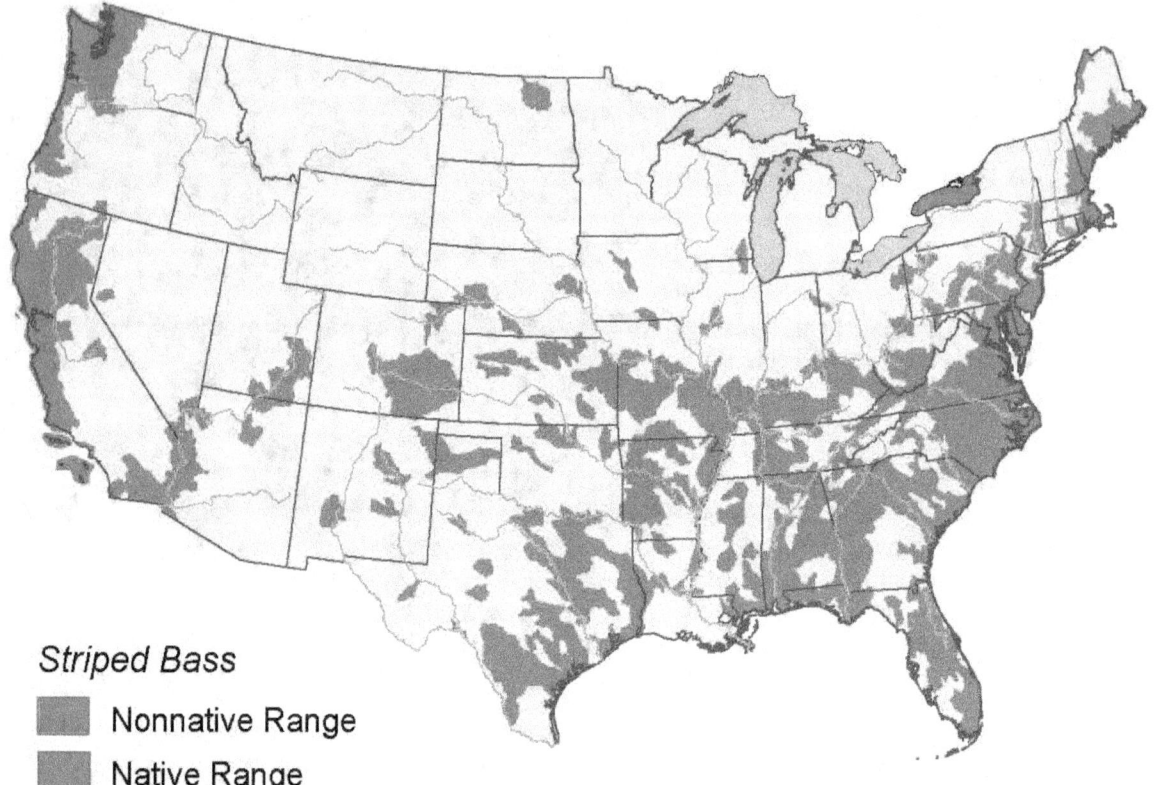

Striped Bass

Nonnative Range

Native Range

Figure 42. Distribution of striped bass *Morone saxatilis* in the United States.

Relation of Habitat and Sampling Method to Fish Catch

Striped bass were first collected by the Long Term Resource Monitoring Program from a side channel in the Open River Reach. Side channels have accounted for 27.1 percent of the 59 fish collected to date. Striped bass were also collected from the main channel (unstructured and wing dam strata combined; 18.6 percent), tributaries (27.1 percent), tailwater zone (23.7 percent), and backwater, contiguous-shoreline (5.1 percent) habitats throughout the Open River and La Grange Reaches. Electrofishing (day and night), gill nets, and fyke nets accounted for 76.3 percent of striped bass collected by the Program (table 10).

Trends in Distribution and Abundance

Total annual catch of striped bass collected by the Long Term Resource Monitoring Program has been irregular and low. The largest annual catch of 16 individuals was collected in 1995 (fig. 44). Striped bass have not been collected outside of the Open River and La Grange Reaches and have not shown an increase in numbers or expansion of their range since 1991 when they were first collected by Program sampling.

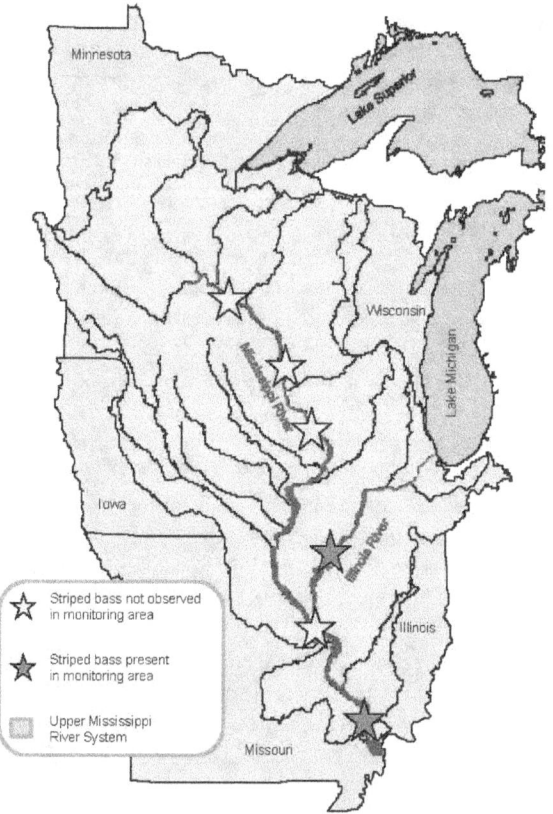

Striped bass not observed in monitoring area

Striped bass present in monitoring area

Upper Mississippi River System

Figure 43. Long Term Resource Monitoring Program study reaches where striped bass *Morone saxatilis* were collected within the Upper Mississippi River System Basin from 1989 to 2002.

Table 10. Striped bass *Morone saxatilis* total catch, by strata and gear, collected by the Long Term Resource Monitoring Program from 1989 to 2002.

[Strata abbreviations: BWC-S, backwater, contiguous-shoreline; MCB-U, main channel border-unstructured; MCB-W, main channel border-wing dams; SCB-O, side channel border-open; SCB-C, side channel border-closed; TRIB, tributary mouth; TWZ, tailwater zone-400 meters below dam. Gear abbreviations: DEF, day electrofishing; F, fyke net; GR, gill net-perpendicular to shore; HL, hoop net-large; M, minnow fyke net; NEF, night electrofishing; S, seine. —, no catch; NA, not applicable]

| | | Gear | | | | | | Total catch, by strata | Percentage of total catch, by strata |
		DEF	F	HL	GR	M	NEF		
Strata	BWC-S	1	2	—	—	—	—	3	5.1
	MCB-U	2	—	—	—	1	—	3	5.1
	MCB-W	6	—	—	—	2	—	8	13.6
	SCB-O	1	—	—	—	1	—	2	3.4
	SCB-C	6	4	2	1	—	—	13	22.0
	TRIB	1		15		—	—	16	27.1
	TWZ	4	2	1		—	7	14	23.7
Total catch, by gear		21	8	3	16	4	7	59	NA
Percentage of total catch, by gear		35.6	13.6	5.1	27.1	6.8	11.9	NA	100.0

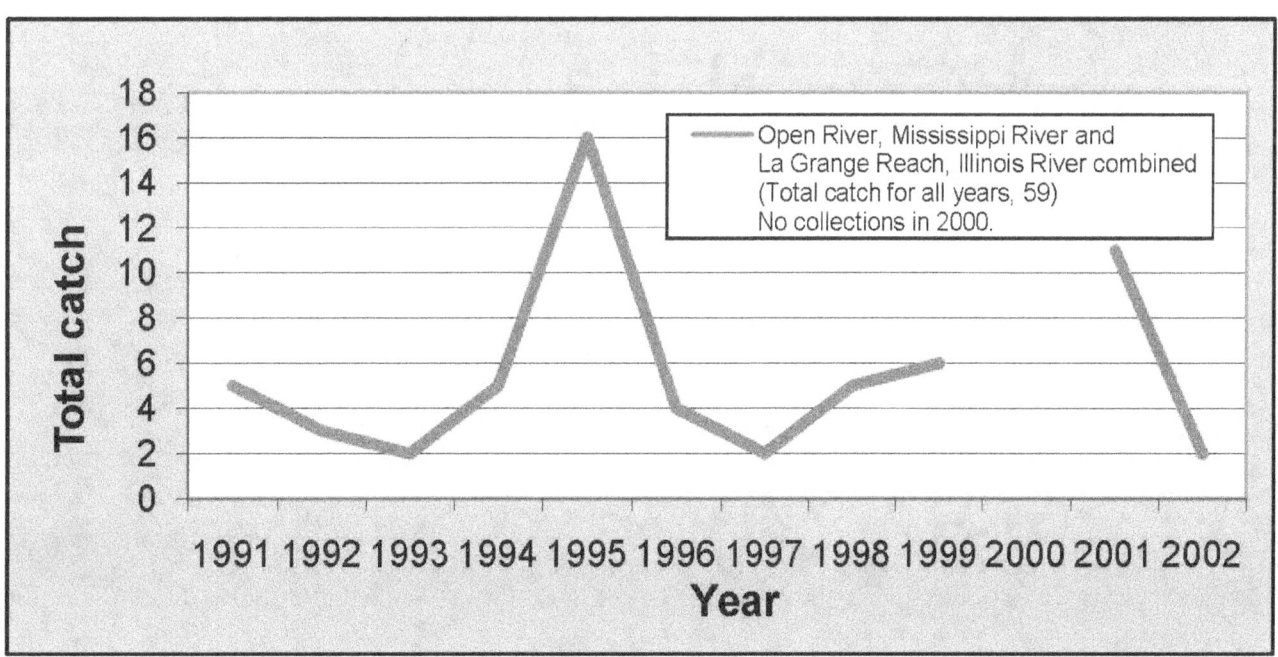

Figure 44. Long Term Resource Monitoring Program total annual catch of striped bass *Morone saxatilis*, all reaches combined, from 1989 to 2002.

Ecological and Economic Impacts

Striped bass are voracious predators as adults and prey heavily on shad and other forage fishes (Stevens, 1965). Hybridization with native white bass has been documented in wild or naturalized populations (Crawford and others, 1984). Striped bass should have few impacts on the fisheries of the Upper Mississippi River System at the low abundances observed to date.

Discussion

Striped bass will not likely have a major affect on the Upper Mississippi River System. The striped bass that do occur in Upper Mississippi River System probably escaped from stocked reservoirs and other impoundments. They also are not likely to successfully recruit because of their specific early life-history requirements. The semibuoyant eggs must flow with the current for as long as 3 days, and this requirement is not generally met in the Upper Mississippi River System. Striped bass are an excellent sport fish noted for their large size, strength, and their nomadic movements over miles of streams, lakes, and estuaries in search of food and habitat (Ross, 2001).

Hybrid Striped Bass x White Bass ("Wiper") *Morone saxatilis* x *M. chrysops*

Photograph by David Ostendorf, Missouri Department of Conservation

Native Range Biology

Artificial hybridization of *Morone* was achieved in 1965 with the production of *M. saxatilis* (striped bass) x *M. chrysops* (white bass) fry. These fish are commonly called "wipers" as well as several other localized names. The subsequent survival of the hybrids was noted within a Tennessee impoundment (Stevens, 1965). The hybrid striped bass x white bass (wiper) was created by crossing a striped bass and white bass to produce a hybrid. Unlike most hybrid fish species, wipers can reproduce in the wild, but only when spawning with one of its two parental species (Ross, 2001). The hybrids resemble their white bass parent, but exhibit faster growth and a shorter life span (Ross, 2001). Adult wipers commonly range from 380 to 508 mm in length and up to 2 kg in weight, with the world record reaching over 10 kg in weight (Etnier and Starnes, 1993; Mettee and others, 1996).

Pathway of Introduction

Wipers have been stocked in more than 30 states (fig. 45), and the greatest numbers are found in the southeastern United States. These populations are artificially maintained. Wipers were first collected in the Upper Mississippi River System by the Long Term Resource Monitoring Program in La Grange Reach in 1993. Wipers have also been collected in Pool 13, Pool 26, and the Open River Reach of the Program. Most are probably escapees from stocked impoundments and reservoirs. Wipers have been stocked in Pool 14 of the Mississippi River since 1984 as part of an experimental hybrid striper stocking program by the Exelon Nuclear Power Plant. At least one tagged fish released in Pool 14 of the Mississippi River has been collected in La Grange Reach of the Illinois River (Illinois Natural History Survey, oral commun., 2002).

Distribution in Long Term Resource Monitoring Program Study Reaches

Hybrid striped bass were collected in four of the six Long Term Resource Monitoring Program study reaches (fig. 46). Of 139 individuals observed in Program collections to date, 4 were collected in Pool 13, 3 were collected in Pool 26, 7 were collected in the Open River Reach, and the remaining 125 individuals were collected in La Grange Reach of the Illinois River. Hybrid striped bass may be more widespread than other hybrids because they are stocked more frequently and stocked directly into the Upper Mississippi River System.

Relation of Habitat and Sampling Method to Fish Catch

Hybrid striped bass was first collected by Long Term Resource Monitoring Program sampling from a backwater area in La Grange Reach of the Illinois River in 1993. However, since that first occurrence, tailwater zones have accounted for 62.6 percent of the hybrid striped bass collected by the Program. Electrofishing (day and night) and fyke nets accounted for 84.2 percent of wipers collected (table 11).

Trend in Abundance

The Long Term Resource Monitoring Program sampling typically results in collection of fewer than 20 hybrid striped bass per year, however, 63 individuals were collected in 1996 (fig. 47). After the peak in 1996, the numbers of individuals decreased and seem to be on a downward trend.

Ecological Impacts

Hybrid striped bass should have few significant impacts on the fisheries of the Upper Mississippi River System. Wipers are often stocked in bodies of water where baitfish are overly abundant to maximize game fish production. Unwanted populations can be eliminated from bodies of water by ceasing to stock hybrid striped bass. Although there is little evidence of interbreeding with white bass in river populations, significant interbreeding between stocked wipers and native white bass stocks could reduce the fitness of white bass throughout the Upper Mississippi River System.

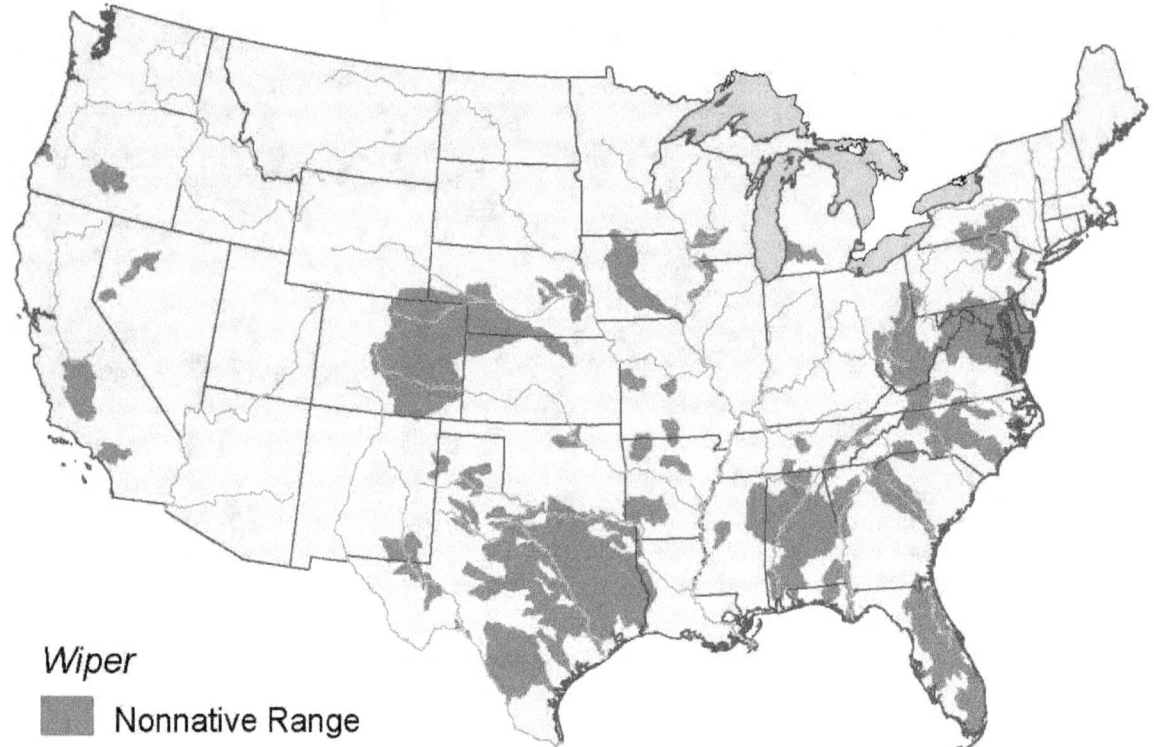

Wiper

■ Nonnative Range

Figure 45.   Distribution of hybrid striped bass x white bass (wiper) *Morone saxatilis* x *M. chrysops* in the United States.

Discussion

Hybrid striped bass will not likely have a major affect on the Upper Mississippi River System. The hybrid striped bass that do occur in Upper Mississippi River System probably escaped from stocked reservoirs and other impoundments or have migrated from Pool 15 stocking efforts. Tagged fish from Pool 15 stocking have found their way into La Grange Reach of the Illinois River and were documented in tag returns (Illinois Natural History Survey, oral commun., 2002). Hybrid striped bass are likely to maintain a minimal presence in the Upper Mississippi River System because of their value as game fish in many of the tributaries that drain into the river system.

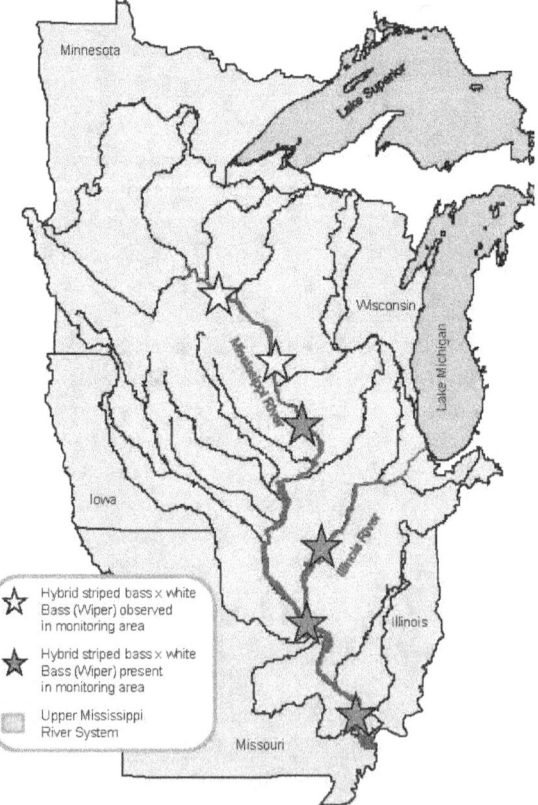

Figure 46.   Long Term Resource Monitoring Program study reaches where hybrid striped bass x white bass (Wiper) *Morone saxatilis* x *M. chrysops* were collected within the Upper Mississippi River System Basin from 1989 to 2002.

Table 11. Hybrid striped bass x white bass (Wiper) *Morone saxatilis* x *M. chrysops* total catch from 1989 to 2002, by strata and gear, collected by the Long Term Resource Monitoring Program.

[Strata abbreviations: BWC-O, backwater, contiguous-offshore; BWC-S, backwater, contiguous-shoreline; IMP-S, impounded habitat-shoreline; MCB-U, main channel border-unstructured; SCB-O, side channel border-open; and SCB-C, side channel border-closed; TWZ, tailwater zone-400 meters below dam. Gear abbreviations: DEF, day electrofishing; F, fyke net; GR, gill net-perpendicular to shore; HL, hoop net-large; M, minnow fyke net; NEF, night electrofishing; S, seine; X, tandem fyke net-offshore. —, no catch; NA, not applicable]

| | | Gear | | | | | | | Total catch, by strata | Percentage of total catch, by strata |
		DEF	F	GR	HK	M	NEF	X		
Strata	**BWC-O**	—	—	—	1	—	—	4	5	3.6
	BWC-S	15	8	1	—	1	—	—	25	18.0
	IMP-S	1	2	—	—	—	—	—	3	2.2
	MCB-U	4	—	—	—	2	—	—	6	4.3
	SCB-O	5	—	—	—	1	1	—	7	5.0
	SCB-C	6	—	—	—	—	—	—	6	4.3
	TWZ	19	10	—	9	3	46	—	87	62.6
Total catch, by gear		50	20	1	10	7	47	4	139	NA
Percentage of total catch, by gear		36.0	14.4	0.7	7.2	5.0	33.8	2.9	NA	100.0

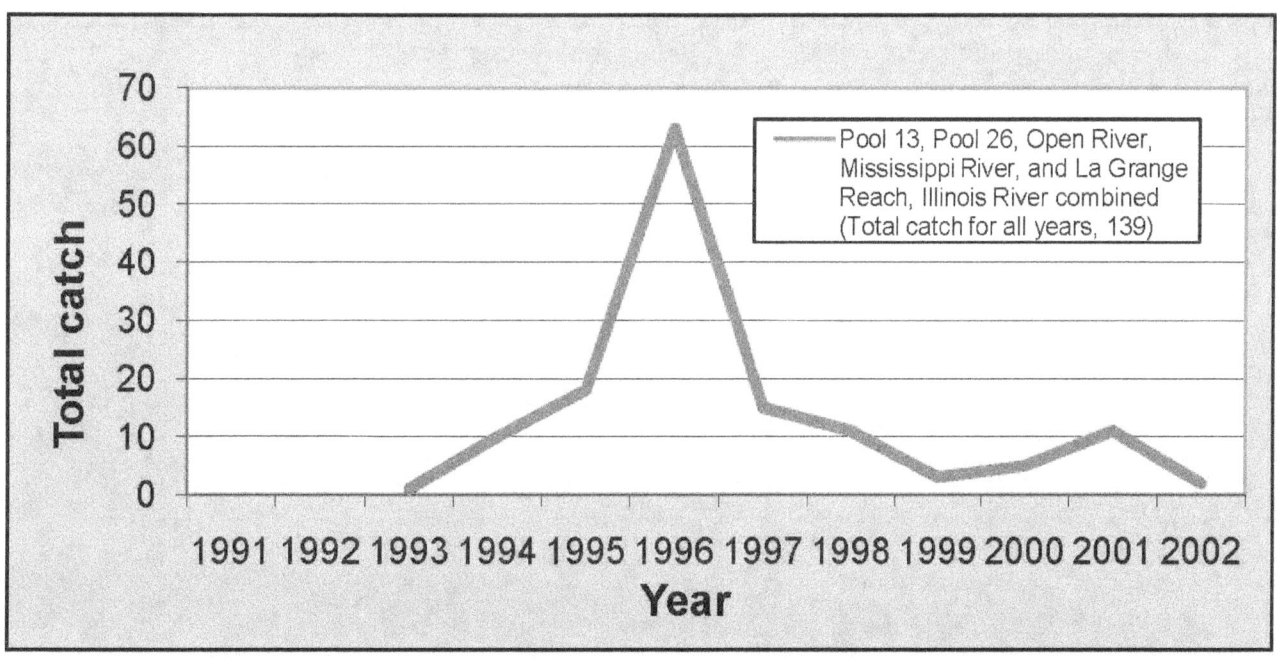

Figure 47. Long Term Resource Monitoring Program total annual catch of hybrid striped bass x white bass (wiper) *Morone saxatilis* x *M. chrysops*, from 1989 to 2002

Figure 48.   Hybrid striped bass (largest, center) surrounded by three white bass in a Long Term Resource Monitoring Program collection. (Photograph by Kevin Irons, Illinois Natural History Survey, Illinois River Biological Station)

References Cited

Allan, J.D., and Felcker, A.S., 1993, Biodiversity conservation in running waters: identifying the major forces that threaten destruction of riverine species and ecosystems: BioScience, v. 43, p. 32–42.

Alvord, J.W., and Burdick, C.B., 1919, Report made to former Rivers and Lakes Commission on the Illinois River and its bottomlands (2d ed.): Springfield, Ill., Department of Public Works and Buildings, Division of Waterways, 137 p.

Bachman, R.A., 1991, Brown trout (*Salmo trutta*) in J. Stolz, and Schnell, J., eds., Trout (The Wildlife Series): Harrisburg, Penn., Stackpole Books Publishers, p. 208–228.

Bailey, W.B., 1975, An evaluation of striped bass introductions in the southeastern United States: Proceedings of the Annual Conference of the Southeastern Association of Game and Fish Commissioners, v. 28, p. 54–64.

Balon, E.K., 1974, Domestication of the carp *Cyprinus carpio* L: Royal Ontario Museum, Life Sciences Miscellaneous Publications, 37 p.

Barnickol, P.G., and Starrett, W.C., 1951, Commercial and sport fishes of the Mississippi River between Caruthersville, Missouri, and Dubuque, Iowa: Illinois Natural History Survey Bulletin 25, p. 267–350.

Bath, D.W., and O'Connor, J.M., 1982, Food preferences of white perch in the Hudson River Estuary: New York Fish and Game Journal, v. 32, p. 63–70.

Bean, T.H., 1897, Notes upon New York fishes received at the New York Aquarium, 1895–1897: Bulletin of the American Museum of Natural History, v. 9, p. 327–375.

Becker, G.C., 1983, Fishes of Wisconsin: Madison, Wis., University of Wisconsin Press, 1,052 p.

Behnke, R.J., 1992, Native trout of western North America: American Fisheries Society Monograph 6, 275 p.

Benson, A.J., Fuller, P.L., and Jacono, C.C., 2001, Summary report of nonindigenous aquatic species in U.S. Fish and Wildlife Service Region 4: U.S. Geological Survey, 142 p., accessed February 2, 2009, at *http://fl.biology.usgs.gov/R5finalreport.pdf*

Berg, L.S., 1964, Freshwater fishes of the U.S.S.R. and adjacent countries (4th ed.): Jerusalem, Israel Program for Scientific Translations, v. 2, 496 p.

Bernstein, N.P., and Olson, J.R., 2001, Ecological problems with Iowa's invasive and introduced fishes: Journal of the Iowa Academy of Science, v. 108, p. 185–209.

Black, J.D., and Williamson, L.O., 1946, Artificial hybrids between muskellunge and northern pike: Transactions of the Wisconsin Academy Science, Arts, and Letters, v. 38, p. 299–314.

Boileau, M.G., 1985, The expansion of white perch, *Morone americana*, in the lower Great Lakes: Fisheries, v. 10, no. 1, p. 6–10.

Buffler, R.J., and Dickson, T.J., 1990, Fishing for buffalo: Minneapolis, Minn., Culpepper Press, 197 p.

Burkhardt, R.W., Delain, S., Kramer, E., Bartels, A., Bowler, M.C., Cronin, F.A., Petersen, M.D., Herzog, D.P., O'Hara, T.M., and Irons, K.S., 2000, 1998 Annual status report: A summary of fish data in six reaches of the Upper Mississippi River System: U.S. Geological Survey, Upper Midwest Environmental Sciences Center, Long Term Resource Monitoring Program 2000–P004, 14 p. plus six chapters [published separately]

Burkhardt, R.W., Delain, S., Kramer, E., Bartels, A., Bowler, M.C., Ratcliff, E., Herzog, D.P., Irons, K.S., and O'Haram T.M., 2001, 1999 Annual status report: A summary of fish data in six reaches of the Upper Mississippi River System: U.S. Geological Survey, Upper Midwest Environmental Sciences Center, Long Term Resource Monitoring Program 2001–P002, 14 p. plus six chapters [published separately]

Burkhardt, R.W., Stopyro, M., Kramer, E., Bartels, A., Bowler, M.C., Cronin, F.A. , Soergel, D.W., Petersen, M.D., Herzog, D.P., O'Hara, T.M., and Irons, K.S., 1998, 1997 Annual status report: A summary of fish data in six reaches of the Upper Mississippi River System: U.S. Geological Survey, Environmental Management Technical Center, Long Term Resource Monitoring Program 98–P008, 15 p. plus six chapters [published separately]

Burkhead, N. M., and Williams, J.D., 1991, An intergeneric hybrid of a native minnow, the golden shiner, and an exotic minnow, the rudd: Transactions of the American Fisheries Society, v. 120, no. 6, p. 781–795.

Burr, B.M., Eisenhour, D.J., Cook, K.M., Taylor, C.A., Seegert, G.L., Sauer, R.W., and Atwood, E.R., 1996, Nonnative fishes in Illinois waters: What do the records reveal?: Transactions of the Illinois State Academy of Science v. 89, nos. 1 and 2, p. 73–91.

Burr, B.M., and Mayden, R.L., 1980, Dispersal of rainbow smelt, *Osmerus mordax*, into the Upper Mississippi River (Pisces: Osmeridae): American Midland Naturalist v. 104, no. 1, p. 198–201.

Cadwallader, P.L., 1977, J.O. Langtry's 1949–50 Murray River investigations: Fisheries and Wildlife Paper 13, 70 p.

Carlton, J.T., 2001, Introduced species in U.S. coastal waters: Environmental impacts and management priorities: Arlington, Va., Pew Oceans Commission, 28 p.

Chang, Y.F., 1966, Culture of freshwater fish in China, *in* Gangstad, E.O., ed., Chinese fish culture. Report 1: Washington, D.C., U.S. Army Waterways Experiment Station, Aquatic Plant Control Research Program, Technical Report A–79. [Draft translated by T.S.Y. Koo, 1980.]

Chick, J.H., and Pegg, M.A., 2001, Invasive carp in the Mississippi River Basin: Science, v. 292, p. ,2250–2,251.

Chilton III, E.W., and Muoneke, M.I., 1992, Biology and management of grass carp (*Ctenopharyngodon idella*, Cyprinidae) for vegetation control: a North American perspective: Reviews in Fish Biology and Fisheries, v. 2, p. 283–320.

Christie, W.J., 1973, A review of the changes in the fish species composition of Lake Ontario: Great Lakes Fishery Commission [United States and Canada], Technical Report Series 23, p. 1–65.

Cochran, P.A., and Hesse, P.J., 1994, Observations on the white perch (*Morone americana*) early in its invasion of Wisconsin: Transactions of the Wisconsin Academy Science, Arts, and Letters, v. 82, p. 23–31.

Courtenay, W.R., Jr., Hensley, D.A., Taylor, J.N., and McCann, J.A., 1984, Distribution of exotic fishes in the continental United States, *in* Courtenay, W.R., Jr., and Stauffer, J.R., Jr., eds., Distribution, biology and management of exotic fishes: Baltimore, Md., Johns Hopkins University Press, p. 41–77.

Courtenay, W.R., Jr., Hensley, D.A., Taylor, J.N., and McCann, J.A., 1986, Distribution of exotic fishes in North America, *in* Hocutt, C.H., and Wiley, E.O., eds., The zoogeography of North American freshwater fishes: New York, John Wiley & Sons, p. 675–698.

Courtenay, W.R., Jr., and Stauffer, J.R., Jr., 1990, The introduced fish problem and the aquarium fish industry: Journal of the World Aquaculture Society, v. 21, no. 3, p. 145–159.

Crawford, T., Freeze, M., Foort, R., Henderson, S., O'Bryan, G., and Phillip, D., 1984, Suspected natural hybridization of striped bass and white bass in two Arkansas reservoirs, *in* Annual Conference Southeast Association of Fish and Wildlife Agencies, 38th, Proceedings: Southeast Association of Fish and Wildlife Agencies, p. 455–469

Crossman, E.J., Holm, E., Cholmondeley, R., and Tuininga, K., 1992, First record for Canada of the rudd, *Scardinius erythrophthalmus*, and notes on the introduced round goby, *Neogobius melanostomus*: Canadian Field-Naturalist, v. 106, no. 2, p. 206–209.

Cudmore, B., and Mandrak, N.E., 2004, Biological synopsis of grass carp (*Ctenopharyngodon idella*): Fisheries and Oceans Canada, Canadian Manuscript Report of Fisheries and Aquatic Sciences 2705, 44 p.

Day, D.M., Sallee, R.D., and Bertrand, B.A., 1996. Changes on goldfish abundance in the upper Mississippi River: Effects of a drought: Journal of Freshwater Ecology, v. 11, no. 3, p. 351–361.

de Iongh, H.H., and Van Zon, J.C.J., 1993, Assessment of impact of the introduction of exotic fish species in northeast Thailand: Aquaculture and Fisheries Management, v. 24, p. 279–289.

De-Shang, L., and Shuang-Lin, D., 1996, The structure and function of the filtering apparatus of silver carp and bighead carp: Acta Zoologica Sinica, v. 42, p. 10–14. [In Chinese with English abstr.]

Dextrase, A., 2001, Surveillance program for ruffe and other exotic fishes: Peterborough, Ontario, Ontario Ministry of Natural Resources, 4 p.

Dill, W.A., and Cordonem A.J., 1997, History and status of introduced fishes in California, 1871–1996: California Department of Fish and Game, Fish Bulletin 178, 413 p.

Emery, L., 1985, Review of fish species introduced into the Great Lakes, 1819–1974: Great Lakes Fishery Commission [United States and Canada], Technical Report Series 45, 31 p.

Etnier, D.C., and Starnes, W.C., 1993, The fishes of Tennessee: Knoxville, Tenn., The University of Tennessee Press, 681 p.

Evans, D.O., and Loftus, D.H., 1987, Colonization of inland lakes in the Great Lakes Region by rainbow smelt, *Osmerus mordax*: Their freshwater niche and effects on indigenous fishes: Canadian Journal of Fisheries and Aquatic Sciences, no. 44, suppl. 2, p. 249–266. [In English with French summary.]

Food and Agriculture Organization of the United Nations, 1999, Aquaculture production statistics 1988–1997 (rev. 11): Rome, Food and Agriculture Organization, Fisheries and Aquaculture Department, Fisheries Circular 815, 203 p.

Fausch, K.D., and White, R.J., 1986, Competition among juveniles of coho salmon, brook trout, and brown trout in a laboratory stream, and implications for Great Lakes tributaries: Transactions of the American Fisheries Society v. 115, no. 3, p. 363–381.

Federenko, A.Y., and Fraser, F.J., 1978, Review of grass carp biology: Interagency Committee on Transplants and Introductions of Fish and Aquatic Invertebrates in British Columbia, British Columbia Department of Fisheries and Environment, Fisheries and Marine Service, Technical Report 786, 15 p.

Forbes, S.A., and Richardson, R.E., 1920, The fishes of Illinois (2nd ed.): Illinois Department Registration and Education, Natural History Survey Division, 357 p.

Freeze M., and Henderson, S., 1982, Distribution and status of the bighead carp and silver carp in Arkansas: North American Journal of Fisheries Management, v. 2, no. 2, p. 197–200.

Froese, R., and Pauly, D., eds., 2004, FishBase: accessed March 2004 at *http://www.fishbase.org*

Fuller, P.L., Nico, L.G., and Williams, J.D., 1999, Nonindigenous fishes introduced into inland waters of the United States: Bethesda, Md., American Fisheries Society Special Publication 27.

Galat, D.L., and Zweimueller, I., 2001, Conserving large-river fishes: is the highway analogy an appropriate paradigm?: Journal of the North American Benthological Society, v. 20, p. 266–279.

Gammon, J.R., and Hasler, A.D., 1965, Predation by introduced muskellunge on perch and bass, I: years 1–5: Transactions of the Wisconsin Academy of Science Arts and Letters, v. 54, p. 249–272.

Greenfield, D.W., 1973, An evaluation of the advisability of the release of the grass carp, *Ctenopharyngdon idella*, into the natural waters of the United States: Transactions of the Illinois State Academy of Science, v. 66, p. 47–53.

Griffith, J.S., 1978, Effects of low temperature on the survival and behavior of threadfin shad, *Dorosoma petenense*: Transactions of the American Fisheries Society, v. 107, p. 63–70.

Günther, A., 1866. Catalogue of the fishes of the British Museum, v. VI: London, British Museum of Natural History, 368 p.

Gutreuter, S., 1997, Fish monitoring by the Long Term Resource Monitoring Program on the Upper Mississippi River System: 1990–1994: U.S. Geological Survey, Environmental Management Technical Center, Long Term Resource Monitoring Program 97–T004, 78 p. plus appendix.

Gutreuter, S., Burkhardt, R., and Lubinski, K., 1995, Long Term Resource Monitoring Program Procedures: Fish monitoring: Onalaska, Wis., National Biological Service, Environmental Management Technical Center, Long Term Resource Monitoring Program 95–P002–1, 42 p. plus appendixes.

Gutreuter, S., Burkhardt, R. W., Stopyro, M., Bartels, A., Kramer, E., Bowler, M. C., Cronin, F. A., Soergel, D. W., Petersen, M. D., Herzog, D. P., Irons, K. S., O'Hara, T. M., Blodgett, K. D., and Raibley, P. T., 1998, 1991 Annual status report: A summary of fish data in six reaches of the Upper Mississippi River System: U.S. Geological Survey, Environmental Management Technical Center, Long Term Resource Monitoring Program 98–P001, 14 p. + Chapters 1–6.

Gutreuter, S., Burkhardt, R. W., Stopyro, M., Bartels, A., Kramer, E., Bowler, M. C., Cronin, F. A., Soergel, D. W., Petersen, M. D., Herzog, D. P., Irons, K. S., O'Hara, T. M., Blodgett, K. D., and Raibley, P. T., 1997a, 1992 annual status report: A summary of fish data in six reaches of the Upper Mississippi River System: U.S. Geological Survey, Environmental Management Technical Center, Long Term Resource Monitoring Program 97–P006, 14 p. + Chapters 1–6.

Gutreuter, S., Burkhardt, R. W., Stopyro, M., Bartels, A., Kramer, E., Bowler, M. C., Cronin, F. A., Soergel, D. W., Petersen, M. D., Herzog, D. P., Irons, K. S., O'Hara, T. M., Blodgett, K. D., and Raibley, P. T., 1997b, 1993 Annual status report: A summary of fish data in six reaches of the Upper Mississippi River System: U.S. Geological Survey, Environmental Management Technical Center, Long Term Resource Monitoring Program 97–P008, 14 p. + Chapters 1–6.

Gutreuter, S., Burkhardt, R. W., Stopyro, M., Bartels, A., Kramer, E., Bowler, M. C., Cronin, F. A., Soergel, D. W., Petersen, M. D., Herzog, D. P., Irons, K. S., O'Hara, T. M., Blodgett, K. D., and Raibley, P. T., 1997c, 1994 Annual status report: A summary of fish data in six reaches of the Upper Mississippi River System: U.S. Geological Survey, Environmental Management Technical Center, Long Term Resource Monitoring Program 97–P007, 15 p. + Chapters 1–6.

Gutreuter, S., Burkhardt, R. W., Stopyro, M., Bartels, A., Kramer, E., Bowler, M. C., Cronin, F. A., Soergel, D. W., Petersen, M. D., Herzog, D. P., Irons, K. S., O'Hara, T. M., Blodgett, K. D., and Raibley, P. T., 1997d, 1995 Annual status report: A summary of fish data in six reaches of the Upper Mississippi River System: U.S. Geological Survey, Environmental Management Technical Center, Long Term Resource Monitoring Program 97–P009, 15 p. + Chapters 1–6.

Hart, J.L., and Ferguson, R.G., 1966, The American smelt: Trade News, v. 18, no. 9, p. 2,223.

Haskell, W.L., 1959, Diet of the Mississippi threadfin shad, *Dorosoma petenense atchafalayae,* in Arizona: Copeia 1959, p. 298–302.

Henderson, S., 1976, Observations of the bighead and silver carp and their possible application in pond fish culture: Little Rock, Ark., Arkansas Game and Fish Commission, 18 p.

Hergenrader, G.L., 1980, Current distribution and potential dispersal of white perch (*Morone americana*) in Nebraska and adjacent waters: American Midland Naturalist, v. 103, p. 404–407.

Hergenrader, G.L., and Bliss, Q.P., 1971,. The white perch in Nebraska: Transactions of the American Fisheries Society, v. 100, p. 734–738.

Herodek, S., Tatrai, I., Olah, J.m and Vörösm L., 1989, Feeding experiments with silver carp (*Hypophthalmichthys molitrix* Val.) fry: Aquaculture, v. 83, p. 331–344.

Hervey, G.F., and Helms, J., 1968, The goldfish: London, Faber and Faber, 271 p.

Hirsch, J., 1998, Nonindigenous fish in inland waters: Response plan to new introductions: St. Paul, Minn, Minnesota Department of Natural Resources, Section of Fisheries Special Publication 152, 21 p.

Hrabik, T.R., Magnuson, J.J., and Mclain, A.S., 1998, Predicting effects of rainbow smelt on native fishes in small lakes: evidence from long-term research on two lakes: Canadian Journal of Fisheries and Aquatic Sciences, v. 55, p. 1,364–1,371.

Hubbs, C.L., 1921, Geographical variation of *Notemigonus crysoleucas*—an American minnow: Transactions of the Illinois State Academy of Science, v. 11 (1918), p. 147–151.

Hurley, D. A., 1992, Feeding and trophic interactions of white perch (*Morone americana*) in the Bay of Quinte, Lake Ontario: Canadian Journal of Fisheries and Aquatic Sciences, v. 49, p. 2,249–2,259.

Irons, K.S., O'Hara, T.M., McClelland, M.A., and Pegg, M.A., 2002, White perch occurrence, spread, and hybridization in the middle Illinois River, Upper Mississippi River System: Transactions of the Illinois State Academy of Science, v. 95, p. 207–214.

Irons, K.S., McClelland, M.A., and Pegg, M.A., 2006, Expansion of round goby in the Illinois Waterway: American Midland Naturalist, v. 156, p. 198–200.

Jennings, D.P., 1988, Bighead carp (*Hypophthalmichthys nobilis*): A biological synopsis: U.S. Fish Wildlife Service, Biology Report 88, p. 1–35.

Johnson, J.E., 1971, Maturity and fecundity of threadfin shad, *Dorosoma petenense* (Günther), in central Arizona reservoirs: Transactions of the American Fisheries Society, v. 100, p. 74–85.

Johnson, T.B., and Evans, D.O., 1990, Size-dependent winter mortality of young-of-the-year white perch: climate warming and invasion of the Laurentian Great Lakes: Transactions of the American Fisheries Society, v. 119, p. 301–313.

Jude, D.J., and DeBoe, S.F., 1996, Possible impact of gobies and other introduced species on habitat restoration efforts: Canadian Journal of Fisheries and Aquatic Sciences, v. 53, p. 136-141.

Kamilov, B.G., and Salikhov, T.V., 1996, Spawning and reproductive potential of the silver carp *Hypophthalmichthys molitrix* from the Syr Darya River: Journal of Ichthyology, v. 36, p. 600–606.

Kimsey, J.B., and Fisk, L.O., 1964, Freshwater nongame fishes of California: California Department of Fish and Game, 54 p.

Kohler, C.C., and Courtenay, W.R., 1986, American Fisheries Society position on introductions of aquatic species: Draft position statement presented at the American Fisheries Society Executive Committee for approval at the 1986 annual meeting.

Kolar, C. S., D. C. Chapman, W. R. Courtenay, Jr., C. M. Housel, J. D. Williams, and D. P. Jennings. 2007. Bigheaded carps: a biological synopsis and environmental risk assessment. American fisheries Society, Special Publication 33, Bethesda, Maryland.

Kolar, C.S., and Lodge, D.M., 2002, Ecological predictions and risk assessment for alien species: Science, v. 298, p. 1,233–1,236.

Krueger, C.C., and May, B., 1991, Ecological and genetic effects of salmonid introductions in North America: Canadian Journal of Fisheries and Aquatic Science, v. 48, p. 66–77.

Kucklentz, V., 1985. Restoration of a small lake by combined mechanical and biological methods: Verhandlungen Internationale Vereinigung für Theoretische und Angewandte Limnologie, v. 22, p. 2,314–2,317.

Laird, C.A., and Page, L.M., 1996, Nonnative fishes inhabiting the streams and lakes of Illinois: Illinois Natural History Survey Bulletin 35, p. 1–51.

Larsen, A., 1954, First record of the white perch (*Morone americana*) in Lake Erie: Copeia, v. 1954, p. 154.

Lazareva, L.P., Omarov, M.O., and Lezina, A.N., 1977, Feeding and growth of the bighead, *Aristichthys nobilis*, in the waters of Dagestan: Journal of Ichthyology, v. 17, p. 65–71.

Lee, D.S., Gilbert, C.R., Hocutt, C.H., Jenkins, R.E., McAllister, D.E., and Stauffer, J.R., Jr., 1980, Atlas of North American freshwater fishes: Raleigh, N.C., North Carolina State Museum of Natural History, 854 p.

Lembi, C.A., Ritenour, B.G., Iverson, E.M., and Forss, E.C., 1978, The effects of vegetation removal by grass carp on water chemistry and phytoplankton in Indian ponds: Transactions of the American Fisheries Society, v. 107, p. 161–171.

Lubinski, K.S., Van Vooren, A., Farabee, G., Janecek, J., and Jackson, S.D., 1986, Common carp in the Upper Mississippi River: Hydrobiologia, v. 136, p. 141–154.

Madenjian, C.P., Knight, R.L., Bur, M.T., and Forney, J.L., 2000, Reduction in recruitment of white bass in Lake Erie after invasion of white perch: Transactions of the American Fisheries Society, v. 129, p. 1,340–1.353.

Maher, R.J., 2002. Commercial catch report exclusive of Lake Michigan: Brighton, Ill., Illinois Department of Natural Resources, Commercial Fishing Program, 20 p.

Master, L.L., Stein, B.A., Kutner, L.S., and Hammerson, G.A., 2000, Vanishing assets: Conservation status of U.S. species, *in* Stein, B.A., Kutner, L.S., and Adams, J.S., eds., Precious heritage: The status of biodiversity in the United States: Oxford, United Kingdom, Oxford University Press, p. 93–118.

Mayden, R.L., Cross, F.B., and Gorman, W.T., 1987, Distributional history of the rainbow smelt, *Osmerus mordax* (Salmoniformes: Osmeridae), in the Mississippi River Basin: Copeia, v. 1987, p. 1,051–1,054.

McGinnis, S.M., 1984, Freshwater fishes of California: Berkley, Calif., University of California Press, 316 p.

Mettee, M.F., O'Neil, P.E., and Pierson, J.M., 1996, Fishes of Alabama and the Mobile Basin: Birmingham, Ala., Oxmoor House, 820 p.

Miller, R.V., 1967, Food of the threadfin shad, *Dorosoma petenense*, in Lake Chicot, Arkansas: Transactions of the American Fisheries Society, v. 96, p. 243–246.

Mills, H.B., Starrett, W.C., and Bellrose, F.C., 1966, Man's effect on the fish and wildlife of the Illinois River: Champaign, Ill., Illinois Natural History Survey Biological Notes 57, 24 p.

Minckley, W.L., and Krumholz, L.A., 1960, Natural hybridization between the clupeid genera *Dorosoma* and *Signalosa*, *with a report on* the distribution of *S. petenensis*: Zoologica, v. 44, 171–180.

Mooney, H.A., and Hobbs, R.J., eds., 2000, Invasive species in a changing world: Washington, D.C., Island Press, 457 p.

Moyle, P.B., 1976, Inland fishes of California: Berkeley, Calif., University of California Press, 405 p.

Nico, L., and Fuller, P., 2001, Grass carp, *in* Nonindigenous Aquatic Species Database: U.S. Geological Survey, *http://nas.er.usgs.gov/queries/FactSheet.asp?speciesID=514* [revision date January 4, 2001], accessed August 1, 2002.

Nico, L., and Fuller, P., 2005, *Scardinius erythrophthalmus*, *in* Nonindigenous Aquatic Species Database: U.S. Geological Survey online database online at *http://nas.er.usgs.gov/queries/FactSheet.asp?speciesID=648.*

Nico, L. G., J. D. Williams, and H. L. Jelks. 2005. Black Carp: Biological Synopsis and Risk Assessment of an Introduced Fish. American Fisheries Society Special Publication 32, Bethesda, Md.. 337 p.

Oehmcke, A. A., Johnson, L., Klingbeil, J., and Winstrom, C., 1965, The Wisconsin muskellunge, its life history, ecology, and management: Wisconsin Conservation Department Publication 225, 12 p.

Omarov, M.O., 1970, The daily food consumption of the silver carp *Hypophthalmichthys molitrix* (Val.): Journal of Ichthyology, v. 10, no. 3, p. 425–426.

Page, L.M., and Burr, B.M., 1991, A field guide to freshwater fishes of North America north of Mexico: New York, Houghton Mifflin Company, The Peterson Field Guide Series, v. 42, 432 p.

Parrish, D.L., and Margraf, F.J., 1994, Spatial and temporal patterns of food use by white perch and yellow perch in Lake Erie: Journal of Freshwater Ecology, v. 9, no. 1, p. 29–35.

Petr, T., 2002, Cold water fish and fisheries in countries of the high mountain arc of Asia (Hindu Kush-Pamir-Karakoram-Himalayas): A review, *in* Petr, T., and Swar, D. B., eds., Cold water fisheries in the Trans-Himalayan countries: Rome, Food and Agriculture Organization of the United Nations, Fisheries and Aquaculture Department, Fisheries Technical Paper 431, p. 1–38

Pflieger, W.L., 1997, Fishes of Missouri (rev. ed.): Jefferson City, Mo., Missouri Department of Conservation, 372 p.

Pimentel, D., Lach, L., Zuniga, R., and Morrisonm D., 2000, Environmental and economic costs of nonindigenous species in the United States: BioScience, v. 50, p. 53–65.

Raibley, P.T., Blodgett, D., and Sparks, R.E., 1995, Evidence of grass carp (*Ctenopharyngodon idella*) reproduction in the Illinois and Upper Mississippi Rivers: Journal of Freshwater Ecology, v. 10, p. 65–74.

Raney, E.C., 1952, The life history of the striped bass, *Roccus saxatilis* (Walbaum): New Haven, Conn., Yale University, Bulletin of the Bingham Oceanographic Collection, v. 14, no. 1, p. 5–97.

Rasmussen, J.L., 2002, The Cal-Sag and Chicago Sanitary and Ship Canal: A perspective on the spread and control of selected aquatic nuisance fish species: U.S. Fish and Wildlife Service, 26 p., accessed February 3, 2009, at *http://wwwaux.cerc.cr.usgs.gov/micra/connectingchannelspaperfinal.pdf.*

Rawstron, R.R., 1964, Spawning of threadfin shad, *Dorosoma petenense*, at low water temperatures:, California Fish and Game. V. 50, no. 1, p. 58.

Reid, W.F., Jr., 1972, Utilization of the crayfish *Orconectes limosus* as forage by white perch (*Morone americana*) in a Maine Lake: Transactions of the American Fisheries Society, v. 101, p. 608–612.

Ricciardi, A., 2001, Facultative interactions among aquatic invaders: Is an "invasion meltdown" occurring in the Great Lakes?: Canadian Journal of Fisheries and Aquatic Sciences, v. 58, p. 2,513–2,525.

Richardson, M.J., Whoriskey, F.G.m and Roym L.H., 1995, Turbidity generation and biological impacts of an exotic fish *Carassius auratus*, introduced into shallow seasonally anoxic ponds: Journal of Fish Biology, v. 47, p. 576–585.

Robins, C.R., Bailey, R.M., Bond, C.E., Brooker, J.R., Lachner, E.A., Lea, R.N., and Scott, W.B., 1991, Common and scientific names of fishes from the United States and Canada (5th ed.): Bethesda, Md., American Fisheries Society Special Publication 20, 183 p.

Robison, H.W., and Buchanan, T.M., 1988, Fishes of Arkansas: Fayetteville, Ark., The University of Arkansas Press, 535 p.

Ross, S., 2001, Inland fishes of Mississippi: Jackson, Miss., University Press of Mississippi, 624 pp.

Sala, O.E., Stuart Chapin, F., III, Armesto, J.J., Berlow, E., Bloomfield, J., Dirzo, R., Huber-Sanwald, E., Huenneke, L.F., Jackson, R.B., Kinzig, A., Leemans, R., Lodge, D.M., Mooney, H.A., 'n Oesterheld, M., LeRoy Poff, N., Sykes, M.T., Walker, B.H., Walker, M., and Wall, D.H., 2000, Global biodiversity scenarios for the year 2100: Science, v. 287, p. 1,770–1,774.

Sanders, L., Hoover, J.J., and Killgore, K.J., 1991, Triploid grass carp as a biological control of aquatic vegetation: U.S. Army Corps of Engineers, Waterways Experiment Station, Information Exchange Bulletin, v. A–91–2.

Savitz, J., Aiello, C., and Bardygula, L.G., 1989, The first record of the white perch (*Morone americana*) in Illinois waters of Lake Michigan: Transactions of the Illinois Academy of Science, v. 82, p. 57–58.

Schaeffer, J.S., and Margraf, F.J., 1987, Predation on fish eggs by white perch, *Morone americana*, in western Lake Erie: Environmental Biology of Fishes, v. 18, p. 77–80.

Schrank, S.J., Guy, C.S., and Fairchild, J.F., 2003, Competitive interactions between age-0 bighead carp and paddlefish: Transactions of the American Fisheries Society, v. 132, no. 6, p. 1,222–1,228.

Scott, D.P., 1964, Thermal resistance of pike (*Esox lucius* L), muskellunge, (*E. masquinongy* Mitchell) and their F1 hybrid: Journal of Fisheries Research Board of Canada, v. 21, p. 1,043–1,049.

Scott, W.B., and Christie, W.J., 1963, The invasion of the lower Great Lakes by the white perch, *Roccus americanus* (Gmelin): Journal of Fisheries Research Board of Canada, v. 20, p. 1,189–1,195.

Scott, W.B., and Crossman, E.J., 1973, Freshwater fishes of Canada: Ottawa, Ontario, Fisheries Research Board of Canada, Bulletin 184, 966 p.

Sheri, A.N., and Power, G., 1968, Reproduction of white perch, *Roccus americanus*, in the Bay of Quinte, Lake Ontario: Journal of Fisheries Research Board of Canada, v. 25, p. 2,225–2.230.

Smith, D.W., 1989. The feeding selectivity of silver carp, *Hypophthalmichthys molitrix* Val: Journal of Fish Biology, v. 34, p. 819–828.

Smith, P.W., 1979, The fishes of Illinois: Urbana, Ill., University of Illinois Press, 314 p.

South Dakota Department of Game, Fish and Parks, 2004, South Dakota 2004 Fishing Regulations, 2004: South Dakota Department of Game, Fish and Parks, *http://www.sdgfp.info/Publications/FishingHandbook.pdf.*

Spataru, P., and Gophen, M., 1985, Feeding behaviour of silver carp *Hypophthalmichthys molitrix* Val. and its impact on the food web in Lake Kinneret, Israel: Hydrobiologia, v. 120, p. 53–61.

Stanley, J.G., Mileym W.W., II, and Sutton, D.L., 1978, Reproductive requirements and likelihood for naturalization of escaped grass carp in the United States: Transactions American Fisheries Society, v. 107, p. 119–128.

Stevens, R.E., 1958, The striped bass of the Santee-Cooper Reservoir, *in*, Annual Conference of Southern Association of Game and Fish Commissioners, 11th, 1957, Proceedings: Southern Association of Game and Fish Commissioners, p. 253–264.

Stevens, R.E., 1965. A report on the operation of the Moncks Corner striped bass hatchery, 1961–1965: Columbia, S.C., South Carolina Wildlife Resources Department, 25 p.

Stokstad, E., 2003, Invasive species: Can well-timed jolts keep out unwanted exotic fish?: Science, v. 301, p. 157–159.

Stolz, J., and Schnell, J., eds., 1991, Trout: Harrisburg, Penn., Stackpole Books, 370 p.

Stone, N., Engle, C., Heikes, D., and Freeman, D., 2000, Bighead carp: Stoneville, Miss., Southern Regional Aquaculture Center Publication 438, 4 p.

Sugunan, V.V., 1997, Fisheries management of small water bodies in seven countries in Africa, Asia, and Latin America: Rome, Food and Agriculture Organization of the United Nations, Fisheries and Aquaculture Department, Fisheries Circular 993, 149 p.

Summerfelt, R.C., Mauck, P.E., and Mensinger, G., 1971, Food habits of carp (*Cyprinus carpio*) in five Oklahoma reservoirs, *in*, Annual Conference of Southeastern Association of Game and Fish Commissioners, 24th, 1970, Proceedings: Southeastern Association of Game and Fish Commissioners, p. 352–377.

Swee, U.B., and McCrimmon, H.R., 1966, Reproductive biology of the carp. *Cyprinus carpio* L., in Lake St. Lawrence, Ontario: Transactions of the American Fisheries Society, v. 95, p. 372–380.

Taber, C.. 1969. The distribution and identification of larval fishes in the Buncombe Creek arm of Lake Texoma with observations on spawning habitats and relative abundance: Norman, Okla., University of Oklahoma, Ph.D. dissertation, 120 p.

Taylor, J.N., Courtenay, W.R., Jr., and McCann, J.A., 1984, Known impact of exotic fishes in the continental United States, *in* Courtenay, W.R., Jr., and Stauffer, J.R., eds., Distribution, biology, and management of exotic fish: Baltimore, Md., Johns Hopkins University Press, p. 322–373

Tennessee Valley Authority, 1954, The shad called threadfin: Tennessee Valley Authority, Division of Forestry Relations, Progress Report for January 1954.

The Upper Mississippi River Management Act of 1986, Public Law 99–662, sec. 1103, U.S. Code 33, chap. 13, statute 652. Thorn, W.C., Anderson, C.S., and Lorenzen, W.E., Hendrickson, D.L., and Wagner, J.W., 1997, A review of trout management in southeast Minnesota streams: North American Journal of Fisheries Management, v. 17, p. 860–872.

Tockner, K., and Stanford, J.A., 2002, Riverine flood plains: present state and future trends: Environmental Conservation, v. 29, p. 308–330.

Tomelleri, J.R., and Eberle, M.E., 1990, Fishes of the central United States: Lawrence, Kans., University Press of Kansas, 226 p.

Trautman, M.B., 1982, The fishes of Ohio (2nd ed.): Columbus, Ohio, Ohio State University Press, 782 p.

Tucker, J.K., Cronin, F. A., Hrabik, R.A., Peterson, M.D., and Herzog, D.P., 1996, The bighead carp (*Hypophthalmichthys nobilis*) in the Mississippi River: Journal of Freshwater Ecology, v. 11, p. 241–243.

U.S. Geological Survey, 1999, Ecological status and trends of the Upper Mississippi River System 1998: A report of the Long Term Resource Monitoring Program: U.S. Geological Survey, Upper Midwest Environmental Sciences Center, Long Term Resource Monitoring Program 99–T001, 236 p.

U.S. Geological Survey, 2004, Nonindigenous Aquatic Species Database: U.S. Geological Survey, Florida Integrated Science Center, accessed at *http://nas.er.usgs.gov/*

Van Oosten, J., 1937, The dispersal of smelt, *Osmerus mordax* (Mitchill), in the Great Lakes region: Transactions of the American Fisheries Society, v. 66, p. 160–171.

Ver Duin, R., ed., 1984, White perch have spread into Lake Huron and Saginaw Bay: The Fisherman, v. 36, p. 16.

Verigin, B.V., Makeyeva, A.P., and Zaki Mokhamed, M., 1978, Natural spawning of the silver carp, *Hypophthalmichthys molitrix*, the bighead carp, *Aristichthys nobilis*, and the grass carp, *Ctenopharyngodon idella*, in the Syr-Dar'ya River: Journal of Ichthyology, v. 18, p. 143–147.

Vörös, L., 1997, Size-selective filtration and taxon-specific digestion of plankton algae by silver carp (*Hypophthalmichthys molitrix* Val.): Hydrobiologia, v. 342, p. 223–228.

Welcomme R.L., 1981, Register of international transfers of inland fish species: Rome, Food and Agriculture Organization of the United Nations, Fisheries and Aquaculture Department, Fisheries Technical Paper 213, 120 p.

Wilcove, D.S., Rothstein, D., Dubow, J., Phillips, A., and Losos, E., 1998, Quantifying threats to imperiled species in the United States: BioScience, v. 48, p. 607–615.

Williamson, M.H., 1996, Biological invasions: London, Chapman & Hall, 244 p.

Xie, P., and Chen, Y., 2001, Invasive carp in China's Plateau Lakes: Science, v. 294, no. 5544, p. 999–1,000.

Xie, P., and Yang, Y., 2000, Long-term changes of Copepoda community (1957–1996) in a subtropical Chinese lake stocked densely with planktivorous filter-feeding silver and bighead carp: Journal of Plankton Research, v. 22, no. 9, p. 1,757–1,778.

Appendix. List of Common and Scientific Names of Fishes

Common name	Scientific name (Genus species)
Paddlefish	*Polyodon spathula*
Bowfin	*Amia calva*
Giant snakehead	*Channa micropeltes*
American shad	*Alosa sapidissima*
Gizzard shad	*Dorosoma cepedianum*
Threadfin shad	*Dorosoma petenense*
Lake herring	*Coregonus artedii*
Brook trout	*Salvelinus fontinalus*
Dolly varden	*Salvelinus malma*
Brown trout	*Salmo trutta*
Rainbow trout	*Oncorhynchus mykiss*
Cutthroat trout	*Oncorhynchus clarki*
Golden trout	*Oncorhynchus aguabonita*
Rainbow smelt	*Osmerus mordax*
Northern pike	*Esox lucius*
Muskellunge	*Esox masquinongy*
Tiger muskellunge x northern pike hybrid	*Esox masquinongy x E. lucius*
Pirapatinga	*Piaractus brachypomus*
Grass carp	*Ctenopharyngodon idella*
Goldfish	*Carassius auratus*
Common carp	*Cyprinus carpio*
Common carp x goldfish hybrid	*C. carpio x Carassius auratus*
Black carp	*Mylopharyngodon piceus*
Silver carp	*Hypopthalmichthys molitrix*
Bighead carp	*Hypopthalmichthys nobilis*
Rudd	*Scardinius erythrophthalmus*
Golden shiner	*Notemigonus crysoleucas*
Bigmouth buffalo	*Ictiobus cyprinellus*
Smallmouth buffalo	*Ictiobus bubalus*
River carpsucker	*Carpiodes carpio*
Channel catfish	*Ictalurus punctatus*
White catfish	*Ameiurus catus*
Western mosquitofish	*Gambusia affinis*
Ninespine stickleback	*Pungitius pungitius*
Inland silverside	*Menidia beryllina*

Appendix. List of Common and Scientific Names of Fishes—Continued

Common name	Scientific name (Genus species)
Black banded rainbowfish	*Melanotaenia nigrans*
Striped bass	*Morone saxatilis*
White bass	*Morone chrysops*
Striped bass x white bass hybrid	*M. chryops x M. saxatilis*
Yellow bass	*Morone mississippiensis*
White perch	*Morone americana*
White perch x yellow bass hybrid	*M. americana x M. mississippiensis*
Largemouth bass	*Micropterus salmoides*
Yellow perch	*Perca flavescens*
Round goby	*Neogobius melanostomus*
Freshwater drum	*Aplodinotus grunniens*